THE ART OF
SHETLAND LACE

Sarah Don

Bell & Hyman Limited

Acknowledgments

Special thanks to Mary Jane Peterson, Mr and Mrs Ritch and their family, Mrs Priest, Mrs Mouat, the curator of Lerwick Museum, Mr Williamson, and his assistant, Mrs Helen Bennett at the National Museum of Antiquities of Scotland in Edinburgh, Mr Kiewe of A.N.I. Limited in Oxford, and Alan who provided most of the photographs in the book.

The author and publishers would also like to thank the Victoria and Albert Museum for supplying the photograph on page 19 and Shetland Museum and Library for the photograph on page 21.

List of Suppliers

STEEL DOUBLE-ENDED NEEDLES UP TO SIZE 16

Stove & Smith, 98 Commercial Street, Lerwick, Shetland.

LEATHER KNITTING BELTS

Goodlad & Goodlad, 90 Commercial Street, Lerwick, Shetland.

YARN

Finest lace weight Shetland yarn (white only) and Shetland lace weight yarn in the natural undyed colours and a number of dyed colours, together with colour card

Jamiesons Knitwear, 93–95 Commercial Street, Lerwick, Shetland.

A.N.I. Ltd., Ship Street, Oxford

Published in 1981 by
Bell & Hyman Ltd,
Denmark House,
37–39 Queen Elizabeth Street,
London SE1 2QB
Reprinted 1982, 1984
© Sarah Don 1980

First published in 1980 by Mills & Boon Ltd

Designed by Richard Brown Associates

British Library Cataloguing in Publication Data
Don, Sarah
   The art of Shetland lace.
   1. Knitted lace—Scotland—Shetland Islands—
   Patterns
   I. Title
   746.2′2041   TT805

Printed in Great Britain by
BAS Printers Limited, Over Wallop, Hampshire
and bound by Hunter & Foulis Limited, Edinburgh
ISBN: 0 7135 2021 3

ONTENTS

Acknowledgments	6	Madeira Wave	52
		Madeira and Diamond	54
List of Suppliers	6	Diamond Madeira and 4-Hole	
		Lace	56
		Lace Cable	60
Introduction	9	Lace Holes	60
		Leaf	62
History of Shetland Lace Knitting	9	Little Leaf Stripe	64
Yarn	16	Eyelid	66
Dressing and Stretching	18	Crown 1	68
Stitch Patterns	20	Crown 2	70
Abbreviations	23	Bead	72
Shetland Knitting Terms and their		Bead Ladder	72
English Equivalents	23	Bead Diamond	74
Basic Stitches Used in Knitted		Hexagon with Spider Pattern	
Lace Patterns	24	Centre, 4-Hole Diamond, Plain	
Basic Techniques in Lace Knitting	25	Hexagon and Waves	76
Typical Shetland Lace Garments	27	Spider's Web, Lace Holes and	
Construction of Shetland Shawls	28	Spider	80
Adapting Garment Patterns	28	Cat's Paw	82
		Arches and Columns	84
		Peerie Flea	86
Samples	31	Diamond and Triangle	88
Fern Lace	32	Rose Lace	90
Fern	34		
Fern and Diamond	36		
Mrs Montague's Pattern	38	Shetland Lace Garments	93
Fir Cone	38	Baby's Shawl in Old Shale Pattern	94
Plain Vandyke Border	40	Hap Shawl in Old Shale Pattern	98
Vandyke Border	42	Baby's Shawl in Several Patterns	100
Trellis Faggot Border	44	Semicircular Scarf in Spider	
Print o' the Wave	46	Pattern	106
Acre 1	48	Scarf in Cockleshell Pattern	108
Acre 2	48	Hap Scarf in New Shale Pattern	110
Madeira Cascade	50	Baby's Christening Dress	112

The beauty of the well known Shetland shawls is, in the minds of most people, associated chiefly with some fashionable shops in the genteeler quarters of London and Edinburgh and it may raise fresh interest to view these tasty items of feminine attire, as adding a grace all their own to the stern shoulders of the fair travellers exploring these regions. I have attempted to depict them decking the rocky lea like gigantic spiders webs and doing their part with dock, buttercup and ragworts in softening the rugged line of the granite strata which stands out from the thin soil in many parts. This is an effect of the operation called shawl dressing. Let us suppose that rain has fallen in torrents for a week past; many hours or even days of assiduous work in spinning, knitting and stitching, occupying the inmates of a group of cottages within, have produced a number of finished fabrics. Dainty white lace shawls with the unusual zig zag stripe—double or treble—the stripe a delicate pink, blue or dove grey on a field of white. Or coarser shawls with black zig zags divided by thin white lines on a field of mouse colour, iron grey or dark brown. But now a fine breezy morning shines upon the Shetland lea, a brisk dying nor'wester brushes over grass and heather. The housewives sally forth with basketfulls of soft white knitting, damp from the wash, and each proceeds to peg down her shawls upon the grass where it is short and free from larger meadow plants such as dock, nettles, etc.

Each shawl requires from 40–50 pegs extended on these at a height of 6 inches above the soil, the wind passing freely above and below and through its many interstices, it strains tighter and tighter as it dries.

Every hour the judicious worker, peg basket in hand, revisits the scene, relaxing or tightening as she readjusts the pegs, till every strong but delicate thread has stiffened into the proper degree of tension, in that geometrical regularity which characterises the whole work. Several hours thus pass till the shawl is properly dressed; it is then methodically folded up and put away and when brought out for sale or exportation it is fit for the bosom and neck of a duchess.

Picturesque Life in Shetland
Frank Barnard

INTRODUCTION

This book is an introduction to the art of Shetland lace knitting—a fully comprehensive coverage of such a subject would deserve an extremely large and weighty volume.

I have included a number of photographs of some of the loveliest pieces of Shetland lace, knitted by Shetlanders engaged in the craft for many years. These are pieces that would have taken years to hand spin and to knit. I hope these will be a source of inspiration to knitters and perhaps a final goal to aim at. Having completed one of the more simple garments from this book I hope you will be inspired to produce your own unique pieces using patterns from this book and other sources. The combinations and arrangements of all the different patterns are never-ending.

History of Shetland Lace Knitting

Sheep have existed on the Shetland Islands since the time of Stone Age man, whose rough stone dwellings can still be seen on the islands. Ancient whorls and spindles have been found on some of these sites providing evidence that spinning was a craft practised even then. There were sheep there when the Vikings arrived in the seventh and eighth centuries A.D. and the Vikings named one of the islands Fair Isle (Isle of Sheep). Because they had to endure poor pastures and appalling weather conditions, only the hardiest sheep could survive and there evolved the softest sheep's wool to be found anywhere in the world. It has a good staple length and it proved to be strong as well as soft, being more suitable for knitting than weaving and so deciding the direction of Shetland's woollen industry which became firmly established as an important part of the economy from as early as the fourteenth century.

When the machine age and mass production swept through Europe and England, the knitting industries were the first to suffer. Knitting and weaving machines practically banished the hand knitting industry and the world of the great knitting guilds came to an end. There was, however, a happier fate for the knitters in the rural areas in the remote and distant countryside, isolated islands and a number of fishing ports around the coastline. Spinning their own yarn from the native sheep and using the natural colours of the wool and their own home dyed colours, women in these areas hung on to their knitting skills which are, even now, providing them with additional income and essential items of woollen clothing.

Patterns gleaned from examples of knitting from all over the world over the years became locally typical, being used over and over again, changed, rearranged and experimented with until each island and each family developed its own distinctive patterns and styles. As the rest of European society rapidly became industrialized, these remote areas retained their family knitting traditions. Apart from the Shetland Isles, including Fair Isle, these consisted of the Hebrides, the Faroes, Scandinavia and the more isolated parts of Spain and Russia, the Channel Islands, and the fishing ports of Britain and Brittany.

9

Most knitwear from these areas fell into the category of essential garments—jumpers and warm clothing once knitted by the men themselves to wear at sea or whilst working on the land or tending their flocks of sheep. Shetland lace garments are the obvious exception, being purely fashionable items of attire, but their making was still essential. The money received for the Shetland lace knitwear was desperately needed for supplies which enabled the Shetlanders to survive during times of hardship. When times were very bad some of the women had to give up working on the crofts altogether to keep their hands in a good enough condition to be able to work full time on the fine lace yarns.

It is believed that the art of lace knitting in the Shetland Isles began a lot later than the coloured patterned knitting known as 'Fair Isle'. By the eleventh century A.D. Spain had become the centre of hand knitted lace and silken hose, and the craft spread rapidly to the rest of Europe. Spanish lace patterns were to greatly influence Shetland patterns. The art of knitted lace must have begun even earlier, some believe in India and perhaps Greece. With the introduction of cotton from India in the 1730s came the craze for 'white work'. The finest white cotton was used to knit lace patterns on the thinnest of wires and domestic knitting reached heights of skill, ingenuity and beauty. Lace knitting became most popular in areas without their own lacemaking traditions such as Britain, Germany, Holland and Scandinavia. However, by the time of the Great Exhibition in 1851, the white lace era was coming to an end, though there were some lovely examples of knitted lace exhibited.

Spanish lace patterns could have arrived in Shetland as early as the fourteenth century via traders involved in the Shetlands' export trade in fish. Nevertheless, although there were many opportunities for samples of lace and knitted lace to have travelled to the Shetlands, especially with the established knitting guilds sending their pupils abroad to learn foreign methods and patterns, it does not seem that there is any evidence to prove that lace knitting was produced in Shetland before 1830, no examples being dated earlier than this time. However, once lace knitting had been introduced, the good staple length and the soft fine quality of the native Shetland fleece must have given great impulse to this new branch of an industry in which the women were already well accomplished.

During Queen Victoria's reign, in the rest of Britain, there were many middle-class ladies madly involved in the creation of anything and everything that could be made for their homes and that could still fall under the heading of 'needlework', a suitable occupation for gentlewomen. In general the standard of this work, done mainly as a pastime, was lower than that in Shetland where it was a means for economic survival. Shetland women were struggling to provide a few extra shillings to buy the urgently needed supplies that could not be produced in their crofts. Many women had to contend with feeding their livestock, helping out on the croft, performing the duties around the home and looking after children—all the time continuing to do their knitting. They did the coarser work by carrying it around with them whilst doing their chores, so urgent was the need for the finished product. The knitting was attached to their waists by means of a knitting belt and safety pins. The best lace knitters, however, were unable to do the chores around the croft since the fineness of the lace yarn demands the very softest

Children's ankle socks in simple lace patterns, knitted on the round, in fine yarn. They were amongst a large number of hand spun, hand knitted lace items found in 1979 during a visit to Unst, in a wooden box at the shop in Uyeasound. The knitting is thought to be 100 years old

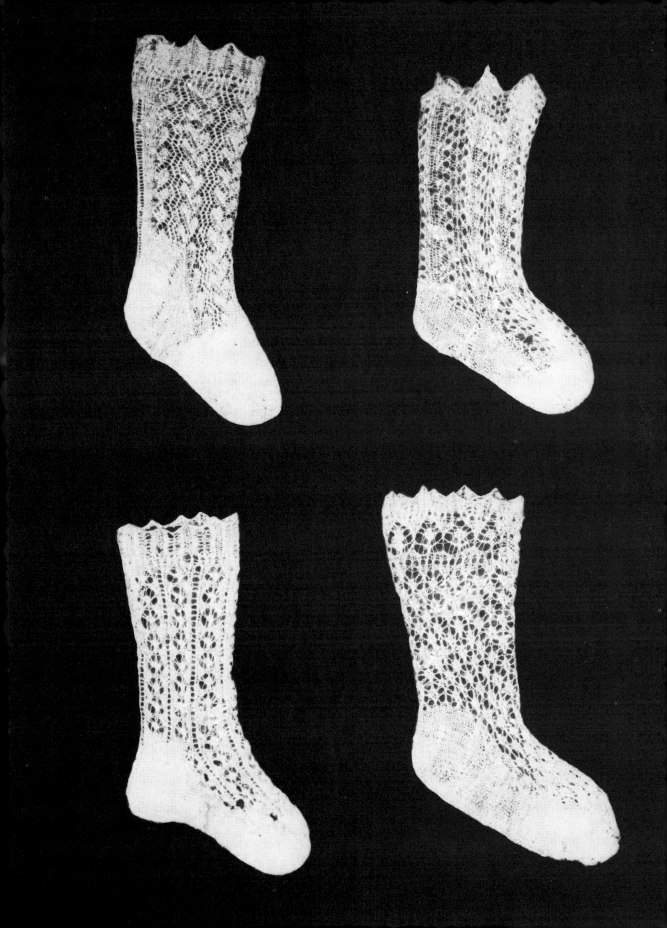

of hands, which must be treated with great care since they are the tools of the trade. It was almost impossible to walk around with the knitting due to its delicacy. In midwinter the sun shines for only a few hours in the day, providing plenty of opportunity for the Shetland women unable to carry out their tasks on the land or crofts to continue with their knitting, so using every moment of their working day.

In 1837 Arthur Anderson tried to popularize Shetland knitwear and presented some fine Shetland stockings to Queen Victoria and to the Duchess of Kent. The hosiery dealer Edward Standen specially commissioned the red and cream wedding veil shown on page 15 for show at the Great Exhibition in London in 1851, hand spun and knitted in Shetland. Edward Standen began to market Shetland knitwear in London and in 1893 the trade was worth £25,000 a year, in 1910 £50,000 and by the year 1920—£100,000. The fine spidery shawls were selling well and were in great demand. They were sold to ladies of the London gentry and were highly prized possessions along with Shetland lace gloves and stockings. In the late nineteenth century a woman could receive £7 10s for making a shawl, though after deducting the cost of the wool she had earnt only 3d to 4d an hour. These beautiful cobweb shawls were made to adorn the graceful shoulders of women from the middle and upper classes, rarely the Shetlanders themselves, for they were items of purely fashionable attire. On the other hand, the Fair Isle and Shetland patterned pullovers, hats, scarves and gloves were the warm, practical and essential items of clothing for the Shetland fishermen.

Some of the knitting had lace edges knitted in dyed purple yarn and shawls could be made in black yarn. (I have included instructions for a semicircular scarf which could by dyed black on page 106.) It seems that black knitting was for wear during mourning, purple for a time after that, and that red was worn at weddings. These colours would have been dyed by the knitter with the aid of the native plants, lichens and minerals, perhaps using the methods used for the Fair Isle colours.

During the First World War the very fine yarn was not produced. Shetland women concentrated their efforts on making sweaters, stockings and other warm clothing for the British soldiers in the trenches and sailors on the high seas. When peace-time came after the armistice, the multicoloured Fair Isle jumper suddenly became popular all over the world, creating an unprecedented demand for work which offered the knitters more money and a quicker return than their lace shawls could bring them. However, during the Second World War lace knitting prospered, mainly due to the fact that many factories in England and Scotland had ceased production of woollens to make munitions. The Shetlanders therefore had little competition and their shawls were sold for £30 to £40 each.

Shetland knitters were taught to knit from the very earliest age, being given needles to play with so that they could mimic their mothers as they knitted. Speeds of up to 200 stitches a minute have been reached with the aid of a knitting belt. This belt is worn around the waist with the right-hand needle inserted into the holes of a pouch stuffed with horsehair. In this way the needle and the work are firmly supported, whilst the forefingers of both hands 'play' the stitches to and from the points of the needles. As the

A bride's veil from the Lerwick Museum complete with headpiece. This was hand spun and knitted by the late Mrs Anne Jane Garrock of Royal Hall, Dunrossness and worn by Mrs M. Sinclair at her wedding in 1910. The borders are made in an extremely complicated design with a simple lace hole centre

knitting grows, it is supported at the left hip by attaching the knitting with a safety pin and a hook from the belt. This also creates the necessary pull on the knitting which is helpful in attaining a fast speed. A Shetland knitter can drop her knitting at any time to see to other business and then return to her knitting without loss of time or stitches! The tension is so well judged that the stitches do not fall off the needle, nor do they break from too tight a tension.

Nowadays machine knitting accounts for 90 per cent of Shetland's knitwear production, but the 'allover' Fair Isle jumpers and fine lace knitting cannot be reproduced by machine. Practically all the yarn used now is factory spun and although there are a small number of women knitting the Fair Isle garments, there are unfortunately even fewer still knitting the fine Shetland lace.

A beautiful wedding veil, an excellent example showing the use of colour. It was made in cream and red stripes—a deep 'royal' red dyed with madder dye and the cream unbleached. It was knitted for Edward Standen & Co. and exhibited by that firm at the Great Exhibition, Crystal Palace, in 1851

Yarn

The first domestic sheep on Shetland were small with brown and cream coloured fleeces moulting every year in spring. Careful breeding over the years has developed strains of sheep with white wool that moults every year and grows continuously. This is an ancient characteristic in breeds such as the Soay, Shetland and Orkney sheep and it means that the wool can be collected at any time, although this is generally done in the summer.

The wool for lace knitting is taken from the neck and back of the sheep, since this is the softest part, and is plucked from the sheep without the fleece being sheared. This is called the 'roo-ing' process. The wool is easily lifted away by the simple method of running the hands along the animal with the fingers spread apart and lifting or roo-ing the wool away.

The combed wool (called 'lemmen') is wound around the finger and then spun using a constant rolling motion between the finger and thumb of both hands against the twist in order to straighten the fibres. Two or three fibres are used to make a single thread. Two of these threads are then wound together in the opposite direction to the original twist so forming the delicate 2-ply yarn. When the spool of spun yarn is full it is coiled on to a wooden reel (a 'niddy noddy') 18 inches long. The fineness of the finished yarn is measured by the number of times the total amount of yarn is wrapped around the reel and is described as being so many threads fine. The thickness of the yarn measured in this way varies from 400 threads to an extremely fine yarn of 1,500 or more threads. This fine yarn is finer than a human hair.

The island of Unst is said to be the home of the Shetland 'ring' shawls, knitted in fine Shetland wool in the natural undyed colours of the native Shetland sheep. They are so fine and gossamer-like that they weigh less than two ounces and although they can measure up to six feet square, they can with ease be pulled through a woman's wedding ring. Mrs Peterson is now the only woman left on Unst spinning the fine yarn required to make the true ring shawls, and she told me that it would take her perhaps a year to spin the one and a half to two ounces of fine yarn needed to knit a ring shawl and another year to knit it. Unfortunately the rest of us will have to be content with using the heavier machine spun 2-ply lace weight yarn which is only available from Shetland (see list of suppliers, page 6) and is sold in half ounce hanks but even this fine yarn may seem a little daunting at first to beginners. Suitable fine 2-ply alternatives to the heavier Shetland lace weight wool used in the patterns for the hap shawl, the scarf and the hap scarf on pages 98, 108 and 110 are available elsewhere from commercial manufacturers.

A typical Shetland spinning wheel used to spin the extremely fine yarn required for the ring shawls.

Photograph by courtesy of the Shetland Museum

Dressing and Stretching

In the time when all Shetland lace was made with hand spun wool, the natural cream colour of the wool needed to be bleached white once a piece of knitting was completed, but before it was washed and stretched. Before the days of chemical bleaches the process was messy and probably dangerous. Live peat was burnt in a barrel or heat-proof crock and rock sulphur was poured over this. The knitting was then suspended over the fire on two sticks and the barrel covered with a lid, the sticks being turned occasionally to prevent the knitting staining. After this the knitting was dipped immediately into a bath of cold water containing small amounts of clothes blue and starch. It was then ready for stretching. This was usually done on a large wooden frame which could be adjusted to accommodate any size of square or oblong. Pegs were placed at intervals of about an inch along the edges of the frame to secure the points of the lace edges by means of stout cotton thread which had been passed through the points of the lace before washing. Frames such as this are still used in the Shetlands. If stretchers were not available, the work would be pegged out on the grass. This stretching process is always necessary to show off the work to its best advantage and to obtain a perfect square, triangle or oblong for shawls and scarves.

WASHING

You will need to wash your knitting once you have completed it as it must be wet, ready for stretching. Make sure all loose ends are secure and woven into the back of your work. Wash in pure soap (not detergent) thoroughly dissolved in lukewarm water. Agitate gently, and then rinse in several changes of clean water at the same temperature (it is sudden changes of temperature in the water that cause wool to shrink and 'felt'). *Do not wring*. Lay work flat on a towel and roll up carefully in the towel to remove excess water.

Note: Every time that a garment is washed the stretching process described here must be repeated. However, these lace garments should not need to be washed frequently.

I would advise you to do your stretching in a room at home where you can be sure there will be no rampant dogs, cats or small children and the knitting can dry completely undisturbed for a day. The best way is to lay a clean sheet over a carpet and pin your work to this using dressmaker's pins (the sort with coloured heads). Do not overstretch at first, but start modestly and move the pins gradually outwards by an inch or so at a time. Mark out the four corners first and with some strong fine thread wrap the yarn around the first pin and tie securely. Now pass the thread around the other pins to outline a square; make sure you have right-angled corners with the aid of a large set square and then pin the work through the holes in the points of the lace on to the sheet in line with the square you have just made. If you wish you may also thread strong cotton through the points of the lace edge before pinning. Both methods will work equally well when stretching your work over a carpet.

A silk cape of the early nineteenth century from the Victoria and Albert Museum. This lovely piece was greatly admired by all the knitters of Unst. It is made using traditional Shetland methods and Shetland patterns, including branches, diamonds of spider stitch and bead stitch, small ferns or Madeiras, diamonds of lace holes, the tree and strawberries, or rooches. The centre is of small ferns or Madeiras and diamond ferns and 4-hole lace —an unusual variation from the puzzle design

Stitch Patterns

When I first began my research into Shetland lace knitting I read that there were only ten truly traditional Shetland lace patterns. When we visited Shetland we realized that there were literally hundreds of patterns, many of them being motifs such as the crown and the tree. With the endless number of variations and the fact that knitters from different families work each pattern in their own way, the result is that no piece of knitting is ever the same. Knitters from these different families also give different names for what is basically the same pattern, so I have not attempted to give names to all of the different patterns, but have named those which do appear to be constant with the Shetland knitters I have talked to. I have also given names to some purely for identification purposes.

The following list of some of the names I came across on Shetland demonstrates how the Shetlanders gave names to those patterns that they could relate to everyday things around them to help identify patterns.

Acre-plough	Ears o' grain	Razor shell
Bawbies' fancy	Fern and roses	Reggies
Bead stitch	Fern lace	Rits
Bird's eye	Fir cone	Shell-cockleshell-wave
Broken leaf	Horseshoe	Shetland eyelet
Cat's eye	Leaf	Shetland fern
Cat's paw	Mrs Hunter's pattern	Shetland twins
Crepes	Old shale	Spider's web
Crest of the wave	Old shell	Spout-ray-shell
Crown of glory	Print o' the wave	Trees

Many of the lace patterns in this book may seem to be extremely complicated but they are in fact, easier to work than most cable patterns and certainly a lot quicker. Due to the fine delicate yarn used for the Shetland lace knitwear, the knitter will need a lot of patience and careful handling of the work. Most mistakes are made by knitting too tightly, which causes the yarn to break, and by casting on too many stitches. Knitted lace is generally very open and stretches a lot whilst being 'dressed'. I cannot stress enough that you must knit samples before embarking on any project, to gain experience and to work out your tension. Many patterns are deceptively intricate and extremely pretty, such as acre, fir cone, razor shell and the very famous and much used old shale pattern. These lace patterns always look much more complicated than they really are. The methods of producing lace are fascinating and once understood, the possibilities are never ending, each pattern having unlimited variations. Having spent much time working out different patterns, I have realized how they have evolved over the years and how many patterns must have come about through very simple errors as well as the careful experimentation by the Shetland knitters!

By delaying increases, placing motifs at 'half drops' and reducing and increasing the number of stitches over which the pattern repeats, many different variations on the same pattern can be achieved. A half drop used in the razor shell pattern becomes fir cone and if the decreases are moved out to the sides on each repeat you make fern lace.

The techniques of working lace stitches can be placed into four different groups: slipped stitches, yarn over stitches, eyelet patterns, faggoting and freehand lace motifs, the latter being the most complicated and in the context of Shetland shawls, it is almost impossible to provide written instructions for them. I leave this task to the most experienced of knitters who may be willing and able to spend the many hours needed to plan and chart these designs.

A fine lace christening shawl over 100 years old and reputedly knitted by Betty Mouat

A baby's christening veil. This must be a unique piece and probably one of the finest ever made, being of the most delicate yarn and knitted on the thinnest of needles over 100 years ago. It was presented to the Lerwick Museum by Miss M. M. Hamilton

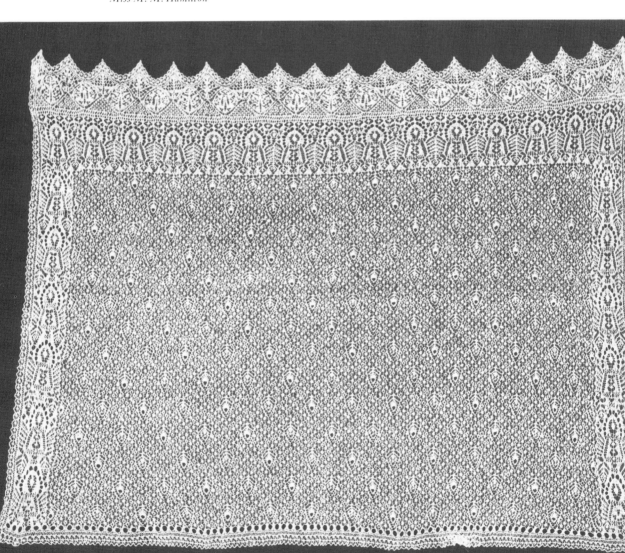

Abbreviations

alt = alternate
foll = following
K = knit
O = wool over
P = purl
2P = pass two slip stitches over
PT = purl two together
rep = repeat
S2 = slip two stitches
SK = slip one stitch knitwise
SKP = slip one, knit one,
pass slip stitch over

SP = slip one purlwise
st(s) = stitch(es)
STP = slip one, knit two together,
pass slip stitch over
T = knit two together
T3 = knit three together
T4 = knit four together
U = make one stitch by picking up
loop between stitches

Shetland Knitting Terms and their English Equivalents

Macking	Knitting
Single macking	Flat knitting
Plain macking	Stocking stitch
Reggies	Garter stitch
Ridge	Two rows of garter stitch
Loop about	Plain and purl
Loops	Stitches
Right loop	Knit stitch
Left loop	Purl stitch
Lay up	Cast on
Cast up	Over
Take in	Decrease
Wires	Needles

Basic Stitches Used in Knitted Lace Patterns

SLIP STITCH PATTERNS

The slip stitch is used to draw stitches up, diagonally across or over the surface of the fabric. It is worked easily and fast. Cast on very loosely when working slip stitch patterns —these cause the fabric to be slightly denser than that produced by other lace stitches.

YARN OVER PATTERNS

Yarn over stitches involve taking the yarn over the right-hand needle and back under before knitting the next stitch, so affecting a single increase. This yarn over is now treated as a single stitch in the following row.

EYELET PATTERNS

These patterns produce a denser and closer fabric than many types of pattern, with openings arranged in various ways on a solid ground. They are best worked in fine yarn and on fine needles to keep eyelets well defined when fabric is stretched and dressed. The eyelets are made with a yarn over and a single decrease. The decrease is the decorative unit. Each eyelet must be separated by at least three rows. If the eyelets are placed closer than this, the pattern becomes a faggoting pattern. The lace holes pattern is a very good example of the use of eyelet patterns. Rows of eyelets are used to separate the borders from the central square in the Shetland shawls.

FAGGOTING

Faggoting is a very basic lace stitch widely used in knitting Shetland lace. This stitch is used to divide and separate patterns, motifs and freehand lace designs. It is a very good idea to practice some of the faggoting patterns to become familiar with the construction of lace patterns. Faggoting involves working a yarn over stitch and a single decrease, but unlike the eyelet patterns only the one pattern row is repeated.

FAGGOT BEADING

Here the pattern is repeated over two rows or more with the increases and decreases being made on the right side rows only. This makes a much more open fabric. The acre is a good example of faggot beading.

FREEHAND LACE MOTIFS

Once the principles of lace knitting and the basic construction of the patterns is understood, it should be possible to create the flowing freehand motifs sometimes used by the Shetland women for their shawls. There is an excellent example in the shawl shown on front cover in conventional tree-like forms. Patterns such as these are reminiscent of the white knitting of the eighteenth and nineteenth centuries. The designs would be best worked out in chart form. Remember to take into account the tension and size of the motifs. (Each square should represent the single stitch for the following row, no matter how the final stitch is formed.)

In Shetland the majority of patterns are worked on a ground of garter stitch though a stocking stitch ground is also used. Most of the less fancy shawls have the central square knitted in garter stitch. However, you may come across English translations of traditional Shetland patterns. These will usually be placed on a ground of stocking stitch.

Basic Techniques in Lace Knitting

CASTING ON

Due to the unique method of construction and design of Shetland lace knitwear there is, in fact, neither very much casting on nor casting off. Most of the edges are picked up or grafted. For the little casting on that there is, it is extremely important that you cast on loosely when knitting lace patterns. There are many different methods of casting on. Whichever method you are most familiar with, always remember that it is the distance between the cast on stitches on the right-hand needle that is the important factor when casting on and not the size of the needles. In Shetland the same size needles are used throughout on a particular piece of knitting. There should be at least one eighth of an inch between each cast on stitch, some patterns will require the casting on to be even looser.

This is the method for casting on that I find most effective:
Make a slip knot a distance away from the end of the yarn, approximately three times the width of the knitting to be done, slip this on to the right-hand needle. The short end of the yarn is held in the left hand, the yarn coming from the ball in the right hand. Draw the short end of the yarn under the forefinger of the left hand and then over it. Insert the needle into front of this loop and knit it off the finger with thread in right hand and on to the needle in the right hand. Adjust the tension of the stitch with the yarn to the correct distance from the first slip knot. Repeat this procedure for the required number of stitches. This method produces a nice neat and elastic edge but should not be used when edges are sewn together or whipped. For this use the common two-needle method making sure you work into the front of the stitches. Do not be tempted to work a plain row before beginning the pattern.

There is a saying in Shetland that the longer the end of the yarn left over after casting on, the longer it will take to complete the garment.

GRAFTING

Note: Remember that the shawl has still to be stretched so all grafted edges must be done loosely, and must have as much stretch as the rest of the shawl.

To graft stitches from two pieces of knitting together follow these instructions:

1 Border to centre square.

Using a large darning needle and yarn and holding needle with stitches from centre square in front of needles with stitches from border in left hand,* slip one stitch from each needle alternately with darning needle and yarn. The yarn must be drawn through *loosely* and evenly. Work to the end and fasten off yarn securely, weaving ends into back of the work. This method creates a line of holes which replaces the row of eyelets made on the first border between the border and the centre square. For the remaining two borders, loops along the edges of the centre square are picked up and placed on a knitting needle (the same number of loops from the centre as there are on the border) and the same procedure is followed as before.

2 If rows of eyelets are knitted at the end of every border this next method of grafting should be used.

Leave stitches on needles and place fabric wrong side up with the needles together and the two pieces of knitting apart. Using a large darning needle and yarn and beginning at the right edge, pass needle up through first stitch of the bottom piece of knitting and up through the next stitch to the left of the first stitch. * Go back to the first stitch of the top piece of knitting and pass the needle down through it and back up through the stitch next to it, to the left. Return to the bottom piece of knitting and pass needle down through the last stitch it came through. Bring up through next stitch on left end of the bottom piece of knitting. Pull yarn to the correct tension (this should be fairly loose). Repeat from * to end. Secure ends and weave into the back of the work. For the remaining two borders and edges of the centre square, loops are picked up from the edge of the square and placed on a knitting needle. They are then grafted as above.

3 Edges of the borders and lace edges.

The corresponding edges of the borders are grafted as follows. With a knitting needle and yarn, begin at corners of the centre and pick up a single loop at a time along the edge of the border. Repeat this procedure for the corresponding edge of the border and graft as before (* to end of paragraph 1). Repeat for the remaining three pairs of edges.

TENSION

Shetland lace knitting should always be worked at a loose tension, especially when using the very finest of yarn, that used for the 'ring' shawl. If you are using this yarn for the first time, you will probably be shocked at its fragility. Do not be put off! After a little practice, nimble fingers will learn to overcome the problem of the yarn breaking.

Before beginning to make your lace garment, and with the needles you will be using for the finished garment, knit samples of all the patterns you will be using over at least 30 stitches.

Follow the instructions for the dressing process and stretch the samples evenly whilst they are drying. When they dry, carefully measure the width and length of each sample and then work out the tension for each sample as follows:

Divide the number of stitches used by the number of inches or centimetres that the sample measures across its width. This will give you the number of stitches needed to make a width of one inch or one centimetre.

Divide the number of rows used for one pattern in the sample by the number of inches or centimetres that the sample measures in length. This will give you the number of rows needed for each inch or centimetre in length.

You will find that each pattern has a different tension, the more open patterns will be larger than the closer ones. It is difficult to change the number of stitches each time you change to a different pattern and often this problem is overcome by the fact that a number of different patterns are used across the piece of knitting at one time. If you find you want to change the pattern completely and the tension is drastically different, you will have to alter the number of stitches on the needle by either decreasing or increasing (as necessary) evenly across the row. However, careful use of patterns and planning of their use should enable you to avoid such action.

Typical Shetland Lace Garments

HAP SCARVES

Hap scarves in the 2-ply lace weight yarn in various colours are very popular at the moment. These are made using patterns which create 'scallops' or 'waves'–patterns such as those on pages 32, 50 and 84.

These scarves can be made in one piece but are usually made in two pieces grafted together in the centre (see page 26). Take care to change colours with the right side facing each time.

Scarves can also be made in the finest lace weight yarn using scalloped patterns such as the Madeira pattern on page 50. (100 stitches on no. 14 needles would create a suitable width.)

LACE SCARVES OR STOLES

The fine lace scarves or stoles are made in three pieces: the lace edge, the straight side of which is grafted to and around the finished work; and a border and half the centre piece which are knitted twice and grafted together in the middle of the centre piece.

Any of the lace edgings can be used around the scarf, and end border patterns and centre patterns can all be chosen from the Samples section. Approximately 90 to 120 stitches, using no. 14 needles and the finest lace weight yarn would be suitable widths.

Construction of Shetland Shawls

Shetland shawls are made in a most ingenious way, with very few cast on and cast off edges. Wherever possible seams are grafted together and stitches are picked up, creating a great amount of elasticity and stretch and at the same time avoiding ugly seams.

The scalloped lace edges are made first, then the borders are made by picking up and knitting loops from the long straight edge of the lace, (approximately one loop or stitch is picked up from every other two of the lace edge). With these stitches the border is knitted towards the centre without shaping for one third of the estimated final length of the border. The decreases are then made at the edges (decrease one stitch at the *end* of *every* row) for the final two thirds of the border. The final width of the border is then the eventual width and length of the centre square. This square is knitted by carrying straight on from the first border with a row of eyelets (* T, O. Repeat from * to end) to divide the border from the centre square.

Three more lace edges and borders are made as the first but usually ending before the row of eyelets. This depends on which method you choose to graft the borders to the centre square (see page 26). These three borders are grafted loosely to the three remaining sides of the centre square. The mitred sides of the borders are then grafted together. All loose ends must be tied and woven carefully into stitches at the back of the work. The shawl is now ready for washing and stretching.

Adapting Garment Patterns

It should not be difficult to use substitute stitch patterns from this book in place of the ones suggested. A little care and planning ahead goes a long way and a competent knitter should not be afraid of experimenting. Only size and shape should remain constant unless you plan to redesign the garment completely.

Note: The stitch patterns described in the 32 samples of the following section could all be substituted for the patterns given in the instructions for making six garments which come at the end of the book (with appropriate adjustments to the number of stitches over which the pattern repeats). None of the stitch patterns found in these instructions duplicate those of the samples.

Diagram 1. The Basic Construction of Scarves and Stoles

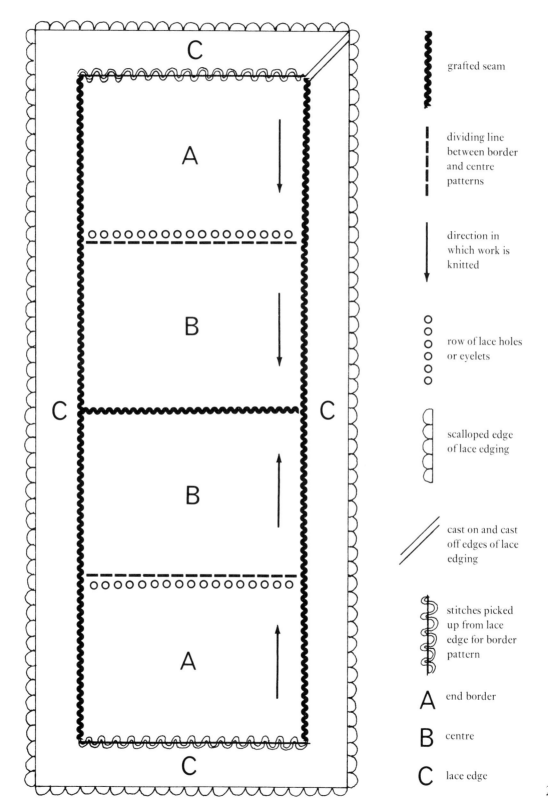

	grafted seam
	dividing line between border and centre patterns
	direction in which work is knitted
	row of lace holes or eyelets
	scalloped edge of lace edging
	cast on and cast off edges of lace edging
	stitches picked up from lace edge for border pattern
A	end border
B	centre
C	lace edge

29

Diagram 2. The Basic Construction of Shawls

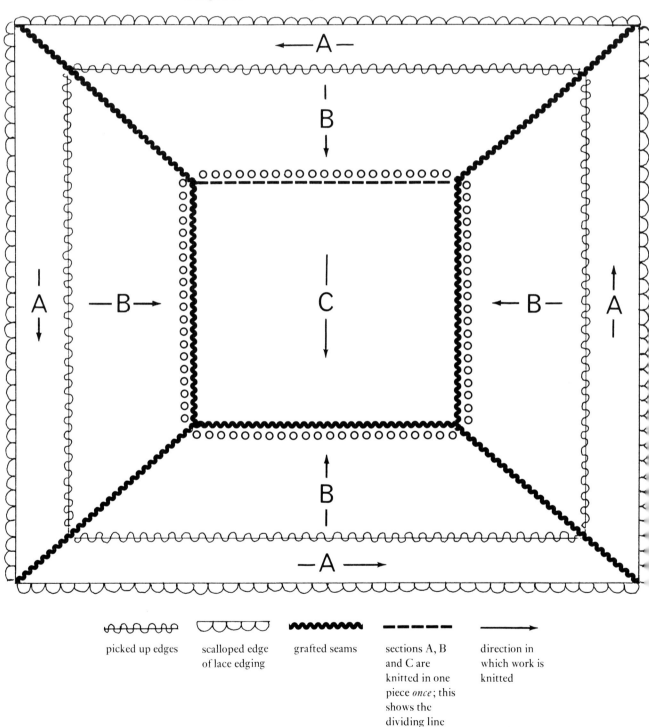

picked up edges

scalloped edge of lace edging

grafted seams

sections A, B and C are knitted in one piece *once*; this shows the dividing line between B and C pieces

direction in which work is knitted

30

SAMPLES

The patterns given in this section can be placed in four groups: lace edgings, 'fill in' or 'allover' patterns and motifs, and scalloped patterns.

The most basic pattern used in Shetland lace knitting is for lace holes. These are made by knitting two stitches together and then making a single increase with a 'yarn over'. Their most obvious use is in the wave patterns. Double lace holes are used in the Baby's Shawl in Several Patterns on page 100 and are made using a double decrease (knitting two stitches together twice) and a double yarn over (which is treated as two stitches on the following row). Lace holes are also used to outline squares, hexagons and other shapes and to divide and separate patterns and borders.

The bead is a good example of how many different ways one pattern can be used. It appears again and again in bead stitch and lace hole edging (Baby's Christening Dress, page 112), bead stitch edging (used in the Baby's Shawl in Several Patterns, page 100), bead, bead diamond and bead ladder.

Motifs such as crown, bead diamond and the tree can be placed singly or arranged in rows, stripes or in groups. The fern or Madeira is one of the most popular motifs and can be used singly or in groups, or for filling spaces between other patterns. In the Baby's Christening Dress on page 112 it is arranged in waves. The fern is also one of the patterns used for the puzzle pattern which appears time and time again in the centres of shawls and stoles. Other 'allover' or 'fill in' patterns are diamond Madeira and 4–hole lace pattern, spider's web, lace holes and spider pattern. Simpler patterns such as leaf, garter stitch, fir cone and Mrs Montague's pattern are usually found in the centres of the heavier weight hap shawls. (Patterns such as the arches and columns, little leaf stripe, new shale, bead, bead ladder and rows 13 to 28 only of the Madeira wave stitch would be suitable for socks, stockings and yokes of dresses.)

Scalloped patterns are put to best use in scarves made of either the finest lace weight yarn or the heavier weight hap yarn. These are patterns such as new shale, cockleshell, Madeira cascade, arches and columns, print o' the wave and fern lace. The old shale pattern is the exception and is probably the most popular Shetland lace pattern. This is used on the borders of shawls (see Baby's Shawl in Old Shale Pattern, page 94).

Fern Lace

Multiple of 18 sts plus 2.

Row 1 and all foll alt rows   P.
Row 2   P2, * K9, O, K1, O, K3, STP, P2. Rep from * to end.
Row 4   P2, * K10, O, K1, O, K2, STP, P2. Rep from * to end.
Row 6   P2, * T3, K4, O, K1, O, K3, O, K1, O, K1, STP, P2. Rep from * to end.
Row 8   P2, * T3, K3, O, K1, O, K9, P2. Rep from * to end.
Row 10   P2, * T3, K2, O, K1, O, K10, P2. Rep from * to end.
Row 12   P2, * T3, K1, O, K1, O, K3, O, K1, O, K4, STP, P2. Rep from * to end.

Rep rows 1 to 12.

Fern

Multiple of 15 sts.

Row 1   K7, O, T, K6.
Rows 2, 4, 6, 8 and 10   P.
Row 3   K5, T, O, K1, O, T, K5.
Row 5   K4, T, O, K3, O, T, K4.
Row 7   K4, O, T, O, T3, O, T, O, K4.
Row 9   K2, T, O, K1, O, T, K1, T, O, K1, O, T, K2.
Row 11   K2, (O, T) twice, K3, (T, O) twice, K2.
Row 12   P3, (O, PT) twice, P1, (PT, O) twice, P3.
Row 13   K4, O, T, O, T3, O, T, O, K4.
Row 14   P5, O, PT, P1, PT, O, P5.
Row 15   K6, O, T3, O, K6.
Row 16   P.

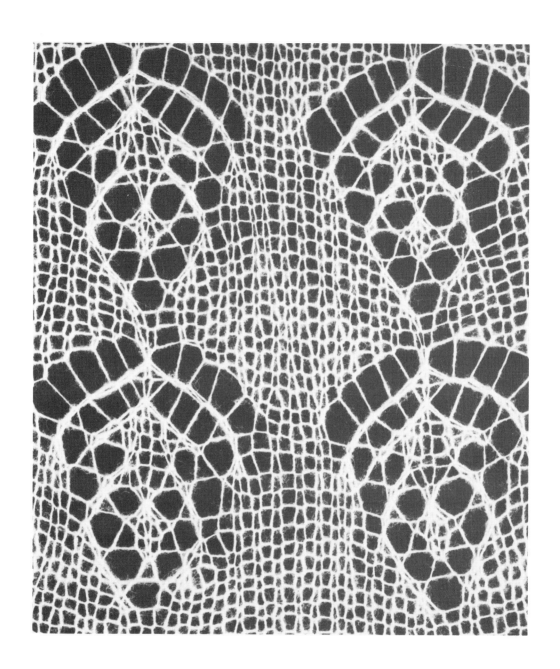

Fern and Diamond

Use a minimum of 52 sts: multiple of 16 sts plus 20 sts for edges.

Rows 1, 3, 5, 7, 9, 11 and 13   K.

Row 2   K2, T, O, * K4, T, O, K1, O, T, K4, O, STP, O. Rep from * to last 16 sts, K4, T, O, K1, O, T, K4, O, T, K1.

Row 4   K6, * T, O, K1, O, STP, O, K1, O, T, K7. Rep from * to last 5 sts, K5.

Row 6   K4, * T, (O, K1, O, STP) twice, O, K1, O, T, K3. Rep from * to end.

Row 8   K5, * (O, STP, O, K1) twice, O, STP, O, K5. Rep. from * to last 4 sts, K4.

Row 10   K7, * O, STP, O, K1, O, STP, O, K9. Rep from * to last 6 sts, K6.

Row 12   K2, * O, T, K5, O, STP, O, K6. Rep from * to last 2 sts, O, T.

Row 14   K2, T, O, * K13, O, STP, O. Rep from * to last 16 sts, K13, O, T, K1.

Row 15   K2, T, O, * K11, O, T, K1, T, O. Rep from * to last 16 sts, K11, O, T, K3.

Row 16   K2, (T, O) twice, * K9, O, T, O, STP, O, T, O. Rep from * to last 14 sts, K9, (O, T) twice, K1.

Row 17   K2, (T, O) twice, * K7, (O, T) twice, K1, (T, O) twice. Rep from * to last 14 sts, K7, (O, T) twice, K3.

Row 18   K2, (T, O) twice, * K9, O, T, O, STP, O, T, O. Rep from * to last 14 sts, K9, (O, T) twice, K1.

Row 19   K2, T, O, * K11, O, T, K1, T, O. Rep from * to last 16 sts, K11, O, T, K3.

Rep rows 2 to 19, ending with one row K.

Mrs Montague's Pattern

Multiple of 16 sts plus 1.

Row 1 and all foll alt rows   P.
Row 2   K1, * K4, O, SKP, K3, T, O, K5. Rep from * to end.
Row 4   K1, * O, SKP, K3, O, SKP, K1, T, O, K3, T, O, K1. Rep from * to end.
Row 6   K1, * K1, O, SKP, K3, O, STP, O, K3, T, O, K2. Rep from * to end.
Row 8   K1, * K2, O, SKP, K7, T, O, K3. Rep from * to end.
Row 10 K1, * K1, T, O, K9, O, SKP, K2. Rep from * to end.
Row 12 K1, * T, O, K3, T, O, K1, O, SKP, K3, O, SKP, K1. Rep from * to end.
Row 14 T, * O, K3, T, O, K3, O, SKP, K3, O, SKP. Rep from * to end.
Row 16 K1, * K3, T, O, K5, O, SKP, K4. Rep from * to end.

Rep rows 1 to 16.

Fir Cone

Multiple of 10 sts plus 1.

Row 1 and all foll alt rows   P.
Rows 2, 4, 6 and 8   K1, * O, K3, STP, K3, K1. Rep from * to end.
Rows 10, 12, 14 and 16   T, * K3, O, K1, O, K3, STP. Rep from * to last 9 sts, K3, O, K1, O, K3, SKP.

Rep rows 1 to 16.

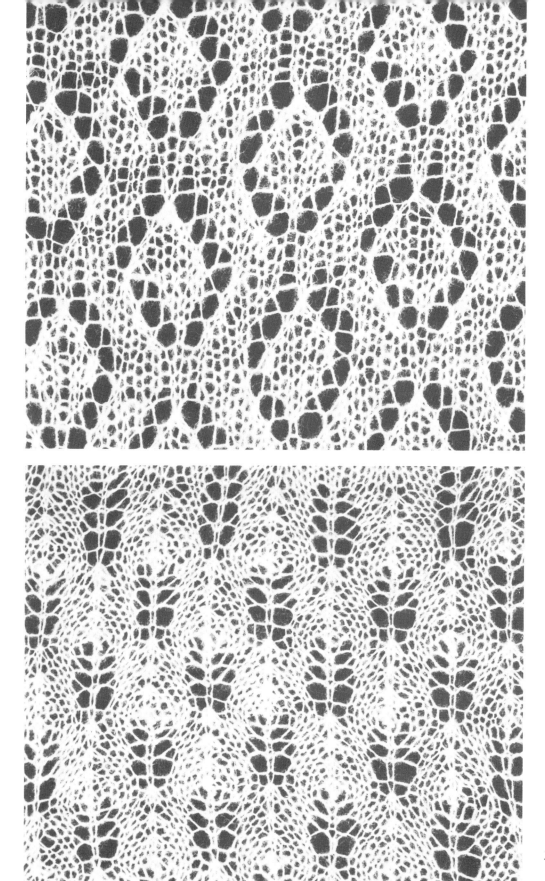

Plain Vandyke Border

Cast on 11 sts.

Row 1 SP, K1, (O, T) three times, O, K3.
Rows 2, 4, 6, 8, 10, 12, 14 and 15 SP, K.
Row 3 SP, K1, (O, T) three times, O, K4.
Row 5 SP, K1, (O, T) three times, O, K5.
Row 7 SP, K1, (O, T) three times, O, K6.
Row 9 SP, K1, (O, T) three times, O, K7.
Row 11 SP, K1, (O, T) three times, O, K8.
Row 13 SP, K1, (O, T) three times, O, K9.
Row 16 K7, (T, O) four times, T, K1.
Rows 17, 19, 21, 23, 25 and 27 SP, K.
Row 18 K6, (T, O) four times, T, K1.
Row 20 K5, (T, O) four times, T, K1.
Row 22 K4, (T, O) four times, T, K1.
Row 24 K3, (T, O) four times, T, K1.
Row 26 K2, (T, O) four times, T, K1.
Row 28 K1, (T, O) four times, T, K1.

Rep rows 1 to 28.

The photograph shows a border knitted in stocking stitch. The instructions are for an alternative version using garter stitch.

40

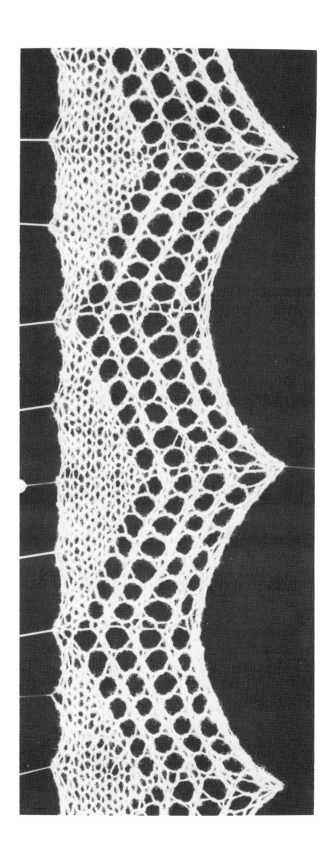

41

Vandyke Border

Cast on 7 sts.

Row 1   K.
Row 2   P.
Row 3   SP, K2, O, T, O2, T.
Row 4   O, K2, P1, K2, O, T, K1.
Row 5   SP, K2, O, T, K4.
Row 6   K6, O, T, K1.
Row 7   SP, K2, O, T, O2, T, O2, T.
Row 8   K2, P1, K2, P1, K2, O, T, K1.
Row 9   SP, K2, O, T, K6.
Row 10 K8, O, T, K1.
Row 11 SP, K2, O, T, (O2, T) three times.
Row 12 (K2, P1) three times, K2, O, T, K1.
Row 13 SP, K2, O, T, K9.
Row 14 Cast off all but 7 sts, K4, O, T, K1.

Rep rows 3 to 14.

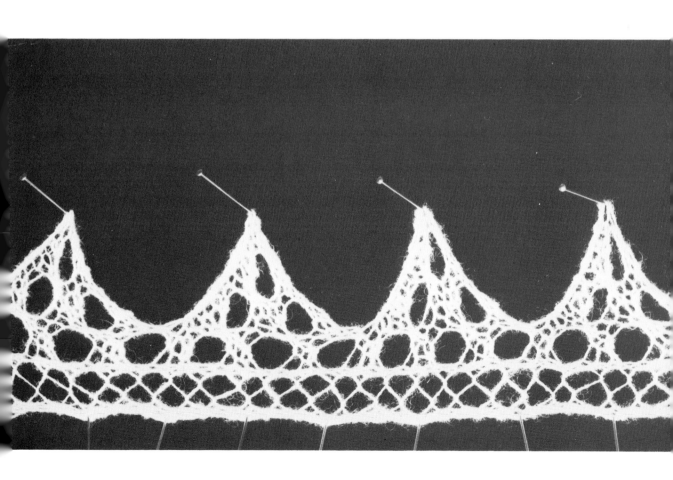

Trellis Faggot Border

Cast on 13 sts.

Row 1 SP, K1, (O, T) twice, K1, O, (SKP, O) twice, K2.
Row 2 and all foll alt rows P.
Row 3 SP, K1, (O, T) twice, K2, O, (SKP, O) twice, K2.
Row 5 SP, K1, (O, T) twice, K3, O, (SKP, O) twice, K2.
Row 7 SP, K1, (O, T) twice, K4, O, (SKP, O) twice, K2.
Row 9 SP, K1, (O, T) twice, K5, O, (SKP, O) twice, K2.
Row 11 SP, K1, (O, T) twice, K2, O, T, K2, O, (SKP, O) twice, K2.
Row 13 SP, K1, (O, T) twice, SKP, O, K1, O, T, K2, (O, SKP) twice, O, K2.
Row 15 SP, K1, (O, T) twice, K2, O, T, K1, SKP, (O, T) three times, K1.
Row 17 SP, K1, (O, T) twice, K4, SKP, (O, T) three times, K1.
Row 19 SP, K1, (O, T) twice, K3, SKP, (O, T) three times, K1.
Row 21 SP, K1, (O, T) twice, K2, SKP, (O, T) three times, K1.
Row 23 SP, K1, (O, T) twice, K1, SKP, (O, T) three times, K1.
Row 25 SP, K1, (O, T) twice, SKP, (O, T) three times, K1.
Row 27 SP, K1, O, T, O, STP, (O, T) three times, K1.
Row 28 P.

Rep rows 1 to 28.

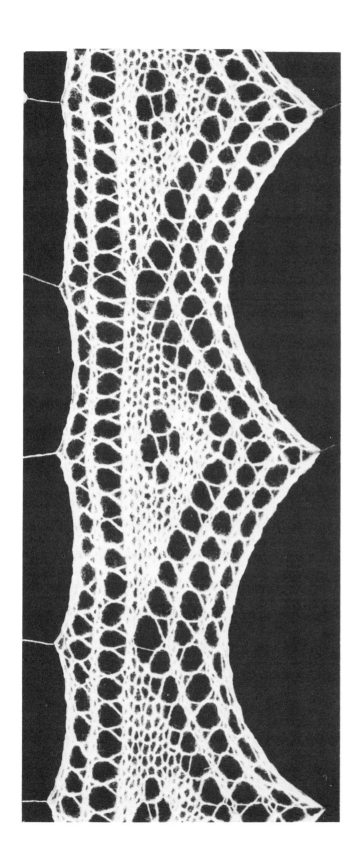

45

Print o' the Wave

Multiple of 22 sts plus 3.

Row 1 K4, * T, K3, (O, T) twice, O, K13. Rep from * to end.
Row 2 and all foll alt rows P.
Row 3 K3, * T, K3, O, K1, (O, SKP) twice, O, K3, SKP, K7. Rep from * to end.
Row 5 K2, * T, K3, O, K3, (O, SKP) twice, O, K3, SKP, K5. Rep from * to last st, K1.
Row 7 K1, * T, K3, O, K5, (O, SKP) twice, O, K3, SKP, K3. Rep from * to last 2 sts, K2.
Row 9 * K12, (O, SKP) twice, O, K3, SKP, K1. Rep from * to last 3 sts, K3.
Row 11 * K7, T, K3, (O, T) twice, O, K1, O, K3, SKP. Rep from * to last 3 sts, K3.
Row 13 K6, * T, K3, (O, T) twice, (O, K3) twice, SKP, K5. Rep from * to last 2 sts, K2.
Row 15 K5, * T, K3, (O, T) twice, O, K5, O, K3, SKP, K3. Rep from * to last st, K1.
Row 16 P.

Rep rows 1 to 16.

Acre 1

Multiple of 10 sts plus 2.

Row 1   P.
Row 2   K2, * O, T, K4, SKP, O, K2. Rep from * to end.

Rep rows 1 and 2.

Acre 2

Multiple of 10 sts plus 2.

Row 1   P.
Row 2   K2, * O, T, K4, SKP, O, K2. Rep from * to end.
Rep rows 1 and 2 four times.
Row 9   P.
Row 10   K3, * SKP, O, K2, O, T, K4. Rep from * to last 3 sts, K3.
Rep rows 9 and 10 four times.
Rep rows 1 to 16.

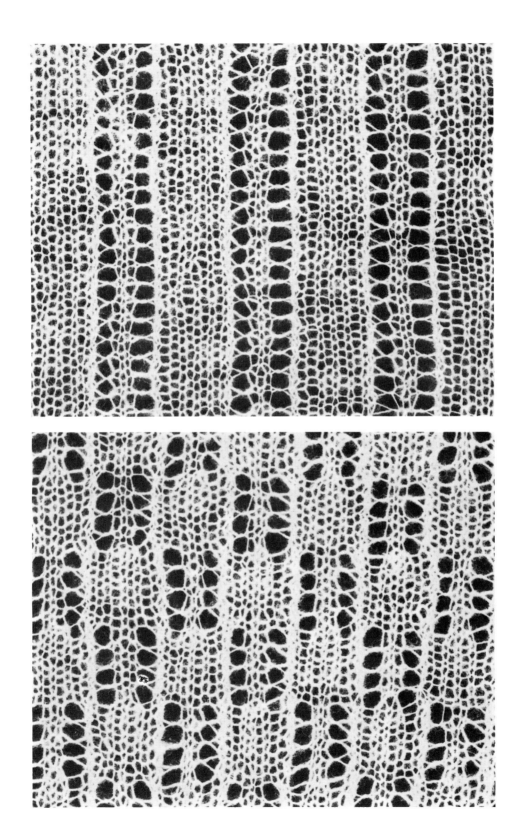

49

Madeira Cascade

Multiple of 20 sts plus 5.

Row 1   K.
Row 2   P.
Row 3   K2, * K1, O, K8, STP, K8, O. Rep from * to last 3 sts, K3.
Row 4 and all foll alt rows   P.
Row 5   K2, * K2, O, K7, STP, K7, O, K1. Rep from * to last 3 sts, K3.
Row 7   K2, T, * O, K1, O, K6, STP, K6, O, K1, O, STP. Rep from * to last 4 sts, O, SKP, K2.
Row 9   K2, * K4, O, K5, STP, K5, O, K3. Rep from * to last 3 sts, K3.
Row 11   K2, * K1, O, STP, O, K1, O, K4, STP, K4, O, K1, O, STP, O. Rep from * to last 3 sts, K3.
Row 13   K2, * K6, O, K3, STP, K3, O, K5. Rep from * to last 3 sts, K3.
Row 15   K2, T, * O, K1, O, STP, O, K1, O, K2, STP, K2, O, K1, O, STP, O, K1, O, STP. Rep from * to last 4 sts, O, SKP, K2.
Row 17   K2, * K8, O, K1, STP, K1, O, K7. Rep from * to last 3 sts, K3.
Row 19   K2, * K1, O, STP, O. Rep from * to last 3 sts, K3.
Row 20   P.

Rep rows 1 to 20.

50

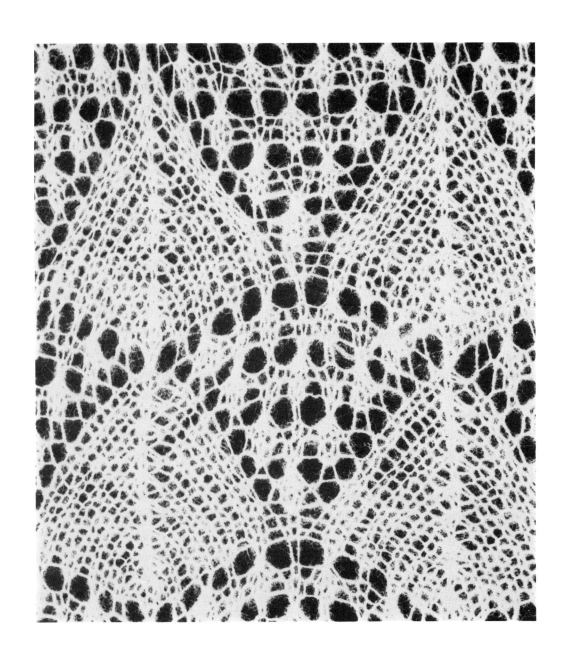

Madeira Wave (described as old Spanish lace pattern)

Multiple of 12 sts plus 5.

Row 1 (right side)   K2, * O, SKP, K10. Rep from * to last 3 sts, O, SKP, K1.
Rows 2, 4, 6, 8, 10 and 12   P.
Row 3   K2, * K1, O, SKP, K7, T, O. Rep. from * to last 3 sts, K3.
Row 5   K2, * K2, O, SKP, K5, T, O, K1. Rep from * to last 3 sts, K3.
Row 7   K2, * K3, O, SKP, K3, T, O, K2. Rep from * to last 3 sts, K3.
Row 9   K2, * K4, O, SKP, K1, T, O, K3. Rep from * to last 3 sts, K3.
Row 11   K2, * K5, O, STP, O, K4. Rep from * to last 3 sts, K3.
Rows 13, 15, 17, 19, 21, 23, 25 and 27   K2, * K2, O, SKP. Rep from * to last 3 sts, K3
Rows 14, 16, 18, 20, 22, 24, 26 and 28   K2, P1, * P2, O, PT. Rep from * to
       last 2 sts, K2.
Rows 29 to 40   Rep rows 1 to 12.
Row 41   K2, * K6, O, SKP, K4. Rep from * to last 3 sts, K3.
Row 42   P.

Rep rows 1 to 42.

Madeira and Diamond

Use 10 sts plus 2.

Row 1 and all foll alt rows K.
Row 2 K2, * O, T, K8. Rep from * to end.
Row 4 K1, * O, STP, O, K7. Rep from * to last st, K1.
Row 6 K3, T, O, * K5, O, T, K1, T, O. Rep from * to last 7 sts, K7.
Row 8 K1, * O, STP, O, T, O, K3, O, T. Rep from * to last st, K1.
Row 10 K3, * (T, O) twice, K1, (O, T) twice, K1. Rep from * to last 9 sts, (T, O) twice, K1, O, T, K2.
Row 12 As row 8.
Row 14 As row 6.
Row 16 As row 4.
Row 18 K1, * K3, O, T, K3, T, O. Rep from * to last st, K1.
Row 20 * K5, O, T, K1, T, O. Rep from * to last 2 sts, K2.
Row 22 K6, * O, STP, O, K7. Rep from * to last 6 sts, O, STP, O, K3.
Row 24 K4, * T, O, K3, O, T, K3. Rep from * to last 8 sts, T, O, K3, O, T, K1.
Row 26 K3, * T, O, K5, O, T, K1. Rep from * to last 9 sts, T, O, K7.
Row 28 K1, * O, STP, O, K3, O, T, K2. Rep from * to last st, K1.
Row 30 K6, * O, STP, O, K7. Rep from * to last 6 sts, O, STP, O, K3.
Row 32 * K5, O, T, K1, T, O. Rep from * to last 2 sts, K2.
Row 34 K2, * K2, O, T, O, STP, O, T, O, K1. Rep from * to end.
Row 36 T, O, * K1, (O, T) twice, K1, (T, O) twice. Rep from * to last 10 sts, K1, (O, T) twice, K1, T, O, K2.
Row 38 As row 34.
Row 40 As row 20.
Row 42 As row 22.
Row 44 As row 24.
Row 46 As row 26.
Row 48 As row 16.
Row 50 As row 18.
Row 52 As row 20.
Row 54 K2, * O, T, K2, O, STP, O, K3. Rep from * to end.
Row 55 K.

Rep rows 4 to 55 as many times as you wish taking the final repeat to row 28.

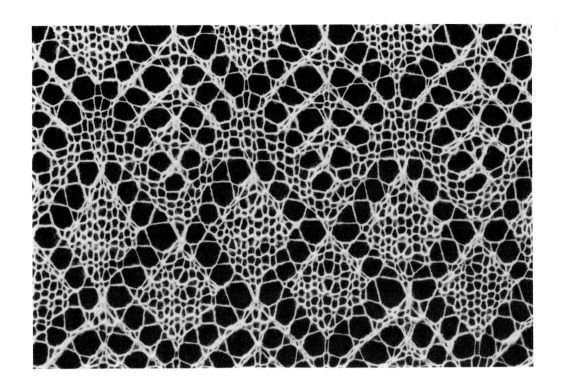

Diamond Madeira and 4-Hole Lace

Multiple of 14 sts plus 1.

Row 1   K5, * T, O, K1, O, T, K9. Rep from * to last 5 sts, K5.

Row 2   K4, * T, O, K3, O, T, K7. Rep from * to last 4 sts, K4.

Row 3   K3, * T, O, K5, O, T, K5. Rep from * to last 3 sts, K3.

Row 4   K2, * T, O, K1, T, (O) twice, T, K2, O, T, K3. Rep from * to last 2 sts, K2.

Row 5   K1, * T, O, K5, P1, K3, O, T, K1. Rep from * to end.

Row 6   T, * O, K1, T, (O) twice, (T) twice, (O) twice, T, K2, O, T3. Rep from * to last 2 sts, O, T.

Row 7   K2, * O, T, K2, P1, K3, P1, T, O, K3. Rep from * to last 2 sts, O, K2.

Row 8   K3, * O, (T) twice, (O) twice, T, K1, T, O, K5. Rep from * to last 3 sts, O, K3.

Row 9   K4, * O, T, K2, P1, T, O, K2, O, T3, O, K2. Rep from * to last 4 sts, O, K4.

Row 10 K5, * O, T, K1, T, O, K2, O, T, K1, T, O, K2. Rep from * to last 5 sts, O, K5.

Row 11 K6, * O, T3, O, K2, O, T, O, T3, O, T, O, K2. Rep from * to last 6 sts, O, K6.

Row 12 K7, * O, K1, O, K2, (O, T) twice, K1, (T, O) twice, K2. Rep from * to last 7 sts, O, K7.

Row 13 K6, T, * O, K1, O, (T, O) three times, T3, (O, T) three times. Rep from * to last 8 sts, O, T, K6.

Row 14 K5, T, * O, K3, O, (T, O) twice, T, K1, (O, T) twice, T. Rep from * to last 7 sts, O, T, K5.

Row 15 K4, T, * O, K5, O, (T, O) twice, T3, (O, T) twice. Rep from * to last 6 sts, O, T, K4.

Row 16 K3, T, * O, K7, (O, T) twice, K1, (T, O) twice. Rep from * to last 5 sts, O, T, K3.

57

Row 17 K2, T, * O, K9, O, T, O, T3, O, T. Rep from * to last 4 sts, O, T, K2.

Row 18 K1, T, * O, K11, O, T, K1, T. Rep from * to last 3 sts, O, T, K1.

Row 19 T, O, * T, K9, T, O, T3, O, T, K9. Rep from * to last 4 sts, T, O, T.

Row 20 K2, * O, T, K7, T, O, K3. Rep from * to last 4 sts, T, O, K2.

Row 21 K3, * O, T, K5, T, O, K5. Rep from * to last 5 sts, T, O, K3.

Row 22 K4, * O, T, K3, T, O, K1, T, (O) twice, T, K2. Rep from * to last 6 sts, T, O, K4.

Row 23 K5, * O, T, K1, T, O, K5, P1, K3. Rep from * to last 7 sts, T, O, K5.

Row 24 K6, * O, T3, O, K1, T, (O) twice, (T) twice, (O) twice, T, K2. Rep from * to last 9 sts, O, T3, O, K6.

Row 25 K4, * T, O, K3, O, T, K2, P1, K3, P1. Rep from * to last 6 sts, O, T, K4.

Row 26 K3, * T, O, K5, O, (T) twice, (O) twice, T, K1. Rep from * to last 5 sts, O, T, K3.

Row 27 K2, * T, O, K2, O, T3, O, K2, O, T, K2, P1. Rep from * to last 4 sts, O, T, K2.

Row 28 K1, * T, O, K2, O, T, K1, T, O, K2, O, T, K1. Rep from * to end.

Row 29 T, * O, K2, O, T, O, T3, O, T, O, K2, O, T3. Rep from * to last 2 sts, O, T.

Row 30 * K1, O, K2, (O, T) twice, K1, (T, O) twice, K2, O. Rep from * to last 3 sts, O, K2, O, K1.

Row 31 K1, O, * (T, O) three times, T3, (O, T) three times, O, K1, O. Rep from * to last st, O, K1.

Row 32 K2, * O, (T, O) twice, T, K1, (T, O) twice, T, O, K3. Rep from * to last 2 sts, O, K2.

Row 33   K3, * O, (T, O) twice, T3, (O, T) twice, O, K5. Rep from * to
last 3 sts, O, K3.
Row 34   K4, * (O, T) twice, K1, (T, O) twice, K7. Rep from * to last 4 sts, O, K4.
Row 35   K5, * O, T, O, T3, O, T, O, K9. Rep from * to last 7 sts, T, O, K5.
Row 36   K6, * O, T, K1, T, O, K11. Rep from * to last 6 sts, O, K6.
Row 37   K5, * T, O, T3, O, T, K9. Rep from * to last 7 sts, O, T, K5.

Rep rows 2 to 37.

Lace Cable

Panel of 18 sts.

Row 1 and all foll alt rows   P.
Row 2   K6, O, SKP, K2, O, SKP, K6.
Row 4   K4, T, O, K1, O, SKP, K2, O, SKP, K5.
Row 6   K3, T, O, K3, O, SKP, K2, O, SKP, K4.
Row 8   (K2, T, O) twice, K1, O, SKP, K2, O, SKP, K3.
Row 10 K1, T, O, K2, T, O, K3, (O, SKP, K2) twice.
Row 12 K3, O, SKP, K2, O, SKP, O, T, O, K2, T, O, T, K1.
Row 14 K4, O, SKP, K2, O, STP, O, K2, T, O, K3.
Row 16 K5, O, SKP, K2, O, SKP, K1, T, O, K4.

Rep rows 1 to 16.

Lace Holes

Multiple of 12 sts.

Row 1   ∗ K4, T, (O) twice, T, K4. Rep from ∗ to end.
Row 2   ∗ K5, K1, P1, K5. Rep from ∗ to end.
Row 3   ∗ K2, T, (O) twice, (T) twice, (O) twice, T, K2. Rep from ∗ to end.
Row 4   ∗ K3, K1, P1, K3, P1, K3. Rep from ∗ to end.

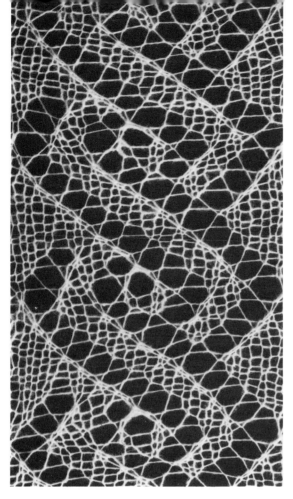

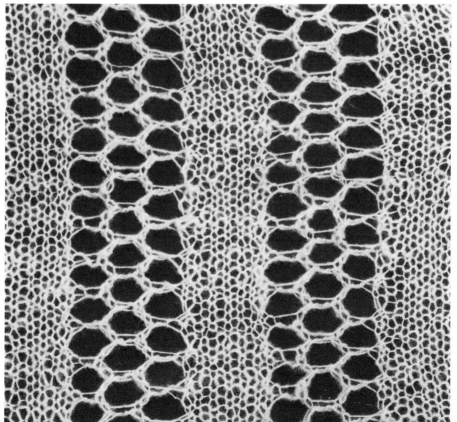

61

Leaf

Multiple of 8 sts plus 1.

Row 1 K1, * O, K2, STP, K2, O, K1. Rep from * to end.
Row 2 and all foll alt rows K.
Row 3 K1, * K1, O, K1, STP, K1, O, K2. Rep from * to end.
Row 5 K1, * K2, O, STP, O, K3. Rep from * to end.
Row 7 K1, * K2, O, K1, O, K2, STP. Rep from * to end.
Row 9 K1, * K1, O, K3, O, K1, STP. Rep from * to end.
Row 11 K1, * O, K5, O, STP. Rep from * to end.
Row 12 K.

Rep rows 1 to 12.

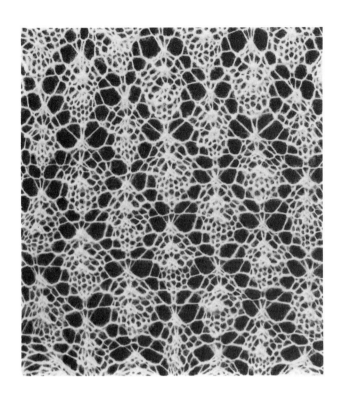

Little Leaf Stripe

Multiple of 8 sts plus 1.

Rows 1 and 3 (wrong side)   P.
Row 2   K1, * T, O, K3, O, SKP, K1. Rep from * to end.
Row 4   K3, * O, STP, O, K5. Rep from * to last 6 sts, O, STP, O, K3.

Rep rows 1 to 4.

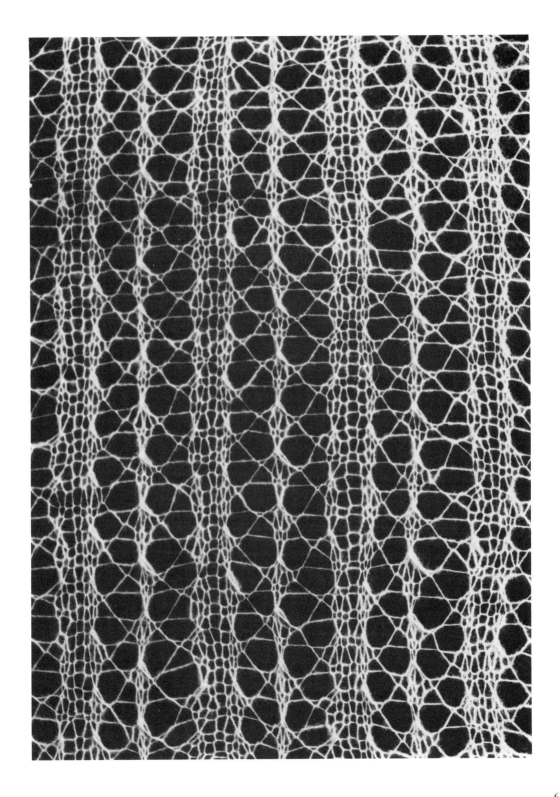

Eyelid

Multiple of 15 sts.

Row 1 K5, T, O, K1, O, T, K5.
Row 2 K4, T, O, K3, O, T, K4.
Row 3 K.
Row 4 K5, O, T, O, T3, O, K5.
Row 5 K.
Row 6 K6, O, T3, O, K6.
Row 7 K.
Row 8 K.

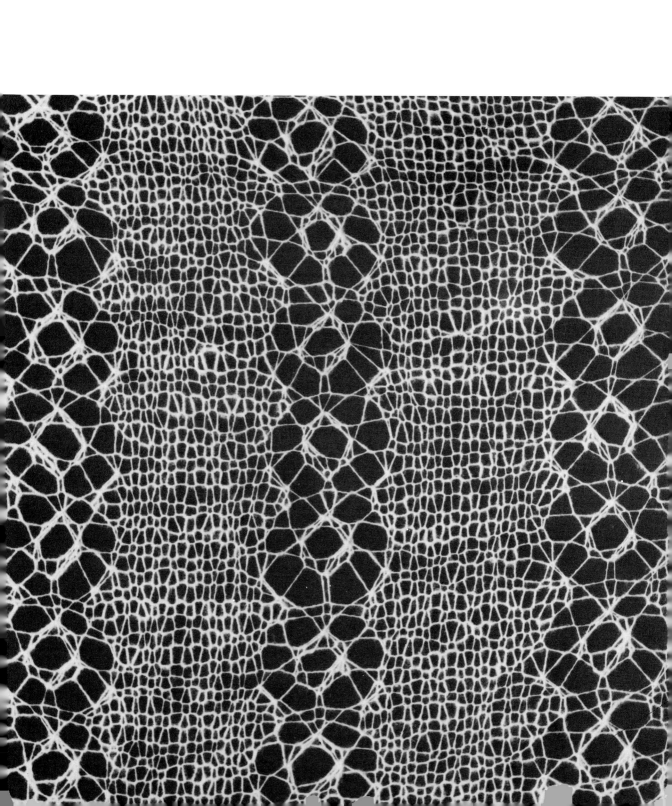

Crown 1

Use 30 sts.

Rows 1, 3, 5 and 7   K.
Row 2   K4, * T, O. Rep from * to last 4 sts, K4.
Row 4   K4, * O, T. Rep from * to last 4 sts, K4.
Row 6   K4, * T, O. Rep from * to last 4 sts, K4.
Row 8   K3, T, O, K21, O, T, K2.
Row 9   K1, T, O, K23, O, T, K2.
Row 10   K1, T, O, K11, O, STP, O, K11, O, T.
Row 11   K2, O, K2, T, K6, O, T, K1, T, O, K6, T, K2, O, K3.
Row 12   K4, O, K2, T, K4, O, T, O, STP, O, T, O, K4, T, K2, O, K3.
Row 13   K4, O, K2, T, K2, (O, T) twice, K1, (T, O) twice, K2, T, K2, O, K5.
Row 14   K5, O, K1, O, K2, (T, O) three times, STP, (O, T) three times, K2, O, K1, O, K4.
Row 15   K2, T, O, K3, O, K2, (T, O) twice, T, K1, (T, O) twice, T, K2, O, K3, O, T, K3.
Row 16   K2, T, O, K5, O, K2, (T, O) twice, STP, (O, T) twice, K2, O, K5, O, T, K1.
Row 17   K1, T, O, K3, T, O, K1, O, K2, T, O, T, K1, T, O, T, K2, O, K1, O, T, K4, O, T, K1.
Row 18   K6, T, O, K3, O, K2, T, O, STP, O, T, K2, O, K3, O, T, K5.
Row 19   K4, T, O, K5, O, K2, T, K1, T, K2, O, K5, O, T, K5.
Row 20   K10, T, O, K1, O, K2, STP, K2, O, K1, O, T, K9.
Row 21   K8, T, O, K3, O, K1, STP, K1, O, K3, O, T, K9.
Row 22   K8, T, O, K5, O, STP, O, K5, O, T, K7.
Row 23   K12, T, O, K3, O, T, K13.
Row 24   K12, T, O, K5, O, T, K11.
Row 25   K10, T, O, K7, O, T, K11.
Row 26   K13, O, T, K3, T, O, K12.
Row 27   K13, O, T, K1, T, O, K14.
Row 28   K15, O, STP, O, K14.
Row 29   K14, STP, K15.
Row 30   K.
Row 31   K.

Crown 2

Cast on 30 sts.

Row 1   K9, (O, T) seven times, K7.
Row 2   K.
Row 3   As row 1.
Row 4   K.
Row 5   K7, T, O, K2, O, K1, T, K3, T, K1, O, K2, O, T, K6.
Row 6   K12, O, K1, (T, K1) twice, O, K11.
Row 7   K6, T, O, K5, O, K1, STP, K1, O, K5, O, T, K5.
Row 8   K13, O, STP, O, K14.
Row 9   K5, T, O, K2, O, K1, T, K7, T, K1, O, K2, O, T, K4.
Row 10 K9, O, K1, T, K5, T, K1, O, K10.
Row 11 K4, T, O, K5, O, K1, T, K3, T, K1, O, K5, O, T, K3.
Row 12 K11, O, K1, T, K1, T, K1, O, K12.
Row 13 K3, T, O, K8, O, K1, STP, K1, O, K8, O, T, K2.
Row 14 K6, T, O, K5, O, STP, O, K5, O, T, K7.
Row 15 K2, T, O, K2, T, O, K1, O, (T) twice, K1, O, K3, O, K1, (T) twice, O, K1, O, T, K2, O, T, K1.
Row 16 K9, T, K1, O, K5, O, K1, T, K10.
Row 17 K1, T, O, K6, T, K1, O, K2, O, STP, O, K2, O, K1, T, K6, O, T.
Row 18 K7, T, K1, O, T, K1, O, K3, O, K1, T, O, K1, T, K8.
Row 19 K2, O, K1, T, K2, T, K1, O, T, K1, O, K5, O, K1, T, O, K1, T, K2, T, K1, O, K1.
Row 20 K2, O, K1, T, K3, T, K1, O, K7, O, K1, T, K3, T, K1, O, K3.
Row 21 K4, O, K1, (T, K1) twice, O, K9, O, K1, (T, K1) twice, O, K3.
Row 22 K4, O, K1, T, K15, T, K1, O, K5.
Row 23 K6, O, K1, T, K5, T, O, K6, T, K1, O, K5.
Row 24 K1, T, O, K3, O, K1, T, K3, T, O, K1, O, T, K3, T, K1, O, K3, O, T, K2.
Row 25 K4, O, T, K2, O, K1, T, K9, T, K1, O, K2, T, O, K3.
Row 26 K4, O, T, K2, O, K1, T, K7, T, K1, O, K2, T, O, K5.
Row 27 K10, O, K1, T, K5, T, K1, O, K9.
Row 28 K5, T, O, K3, O, K1, T, K3, T, K1, O, K3, O, T, K6.
Row 29 K8, O, T, K2, O, K1, (T, K1) twice, O, K2, T, O, K7.

Row 30 K14, O, STP, O, K13.
Row 31 K9, T, O, K7, O, T, K10.
Row 32 K12, O, STP, O, K1, O, STP, O, K11.
Row 33 K12, O, T, K1, T, O, K13.
Row 34 K13, T, O, K1, O, T, K12.
Row 35 K11, T, O, K3, O, T, K12.
Row 36 K12, T, O, K3, O, T, K11.
Row 37 K12, O, T, K1, T, O, K13.
Row 38 K14, O, STP, O, K13.
Row 39 K.

Bead

Multiple of 6 sts plus 1.

Row 1 K2, * O, STP, O, K3. Rep from * to last 5 sts, O, STP, O, K2.
Row 2 K1, T, * O, K1, O, T, K1, T. Rep from * to last 4 sts, O, K1, O, T, K1.
Row 3 T, O, * K3, O, STP, O. Rep from * to last 5 sts, K3, O, T.
Row 4 K1, O, T, K1, * T, O, K1, O, T, K1. Rep from * to last 3 sts, T, O, K1.

Bead Ladder

Multiple of 6 sts plus 1.

Row 1 K1, * T, O, K1, O, T, K1. Rep from * to end.
Row 2 K1, * O, T, K1, T, O, K1. Rep from * to end.
Row 3 T, O, K3, * O, STP, O, K3. Rep from * to last 2 sts, O, T.
Row 4 K1, * T, O, K1, O, T, K1. Rep from * to end.

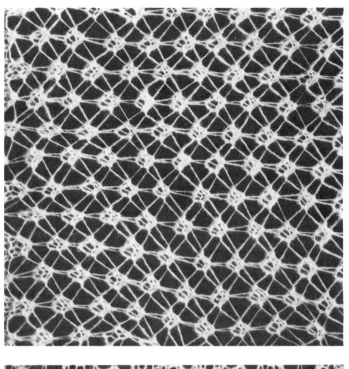

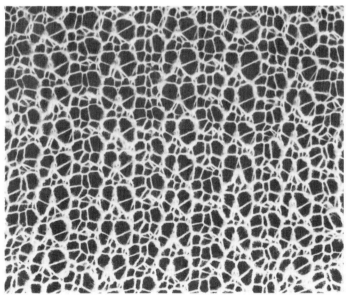

Bead Diamond

Cast on 15 sts and work at least 2 rows in K before beginning the pattern.

Row 1   K5, T, O, K1, O, T, K5.
Row 2   K4, T, O, K3, O, T, K4.
Row 3   K2, T, O, K1, O, T, K1, T, O, K1, O, T, K2.
Row 4   K1, T, O, K3, O, T3, O, K3, O, T, K1.
Row 5   K2, O, T, K1, T, O, K1, O, T, K1, T, O, K2.
Row 6   K3, O, T3, O, K3, O, T3, O, K3.
Row 7   K5, O, T, K1, T, O, K5.
Row 8   K6, O, T3, O, K6.
Rows 9 to 14   K.

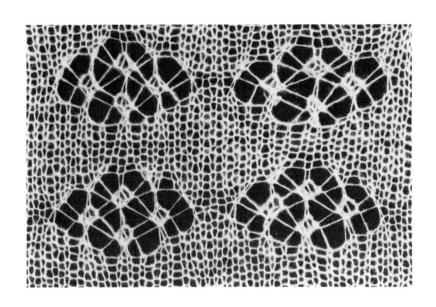

Hexagon with Spider Pattern Centre, 4-Hole Diamond, Plain Hexagon and Waves

HEXAGON WITH SPIDER PATTERN CENTRE

Multiple of 23 sts plus 1.

Row 1 K12, T, * O, K1, O, T, K15, T. Rep from * to last 14 sts, O, T, K12.
Row 2 K11, T, * O, K3, O, T, K13, T. Rep from * to last 13 sts, O, T, K11.
Row 3 K10, T, * O, K5, O, T, K11, T. Rep from * to last 12 sts, O, T, K10.
Row 4 K9, T, * O, K7, O, T, K9, T. Rep from * to last 11 sts, O, T, K9.
Row 5 K8, T, * O, K9, O, T, K7, T. Rep from * to last 10 sts, O, T, K8.
Row 6 K7, T, * O, K11, O, T, K5, T. Rep from * to last 9 sts, O, T, K7.
Row 7 K6, T, * O, K13, O, T, K3, T. Rep from * to last 8 sts, O, T, K6.
Row 8 K5, T, * O, K15, O, T, K1, T. Rep from * to last 7 sts, O, T, K5.
Row 9 K4, T, * O, K17, O, T3. Rep from * to last 6 sts, O, T, K4.
Row 10 K3, T, * O, T, K5, T, O, K1, O, T, K5, T, O, K1. Rep from * to last 5 sts, O, T, K3.
Row 11 K4, * O, T, K15, T, O, K1. Rep from * to last 4 sts, O, K4.
Row 12 K4, * O, T, K4, T, O, K3, O, T, K4, T, O, K1. Rep from * to last 4 sts, O, K4.
Row 13 K4, * O, T, K15, T, O, K1. Rep from * to last 4 sts, O, K4.
Row 14 K4, * O, T, K2, T, O, K1, O, T, O, T3, O, K1, O, T, K2, T, O, K1. Rep from * to last 4 sts, O, K4.
Rows 15, 17, 19, 21 and 23 As row 11.
Row 16 K4, * O, T, K1, T, O, K3, O, T3, O, K3, O, T, K1, T, O, K1. Rep from * to last 4 sts, O, K4.
Row 18 K4, * O, T, K2, O, T, O, T3, O, K1, O, T, O, T3, O, K2, T, O, K1. Rep from * to last 4 sts, O, K4.
Row 20 K4, * O, T, K3, O, T3, O, K3, O, T3, O, K3, T, O, K1. Rep from * to last 4 sts, O, K4.
Row 22 K4, * O, T, K5, O, T, O, T3, O, K5, T, O, K1. Rep from * to last 4 sts, O, K4.
Row 24 K4, * O, T, K6, O, T3, O, K6, T, O, K1. Rep from * to last 4 sts, O, K4.
Row 25 K5, * O, T, K13, T, O, K3. Rep from * to last 5 sts, O, K5.
Row 26 K6, * O, T, K11, T, O, K5. Rep from * to last 6 sts, O, K6.
Row 27 K7, * O, T, K9, T, O, K7. Rep from * to last 7 sts, O, K7.
Row 28 K8, * O, T, K7, T, O, K9. Rep from * to last 8 sts, O, K8.
Row 29 K9, * O, T, K5, T, O, K11. Rep from * to last 9 sts, O, K9.
Row 30 K10, * O, T, K3, T, O, K13. Rep from * to last 10 sts, O, K10.
Row 31 K11, * O, T, K1, T, O, K15. Rep from * to last 11 sts, O, K11.
Row 32 K12, * O, T3, O, K17. Rep from * to last 12 sts, O, K12.

4-HOLE DIAMOND

Multiple of 14 sts plus 1.

Row 1   K5, T, * O, K1, O, T, K9, T. Rep from * to last 7 sts, O, T, K5.
Row 2   K4, T, * O, K3, O, T, K7, T. Rep from * to last 6 sts, O, T, K4.
Row 3   K3, T, * O, K5, O, T, K5, T. Rep from * to last 5 sts, O, T, K3.
Row 4   K2, T, * O, K1, T, (O) twice, T, K2, O, T, K3, T. Rep from * to last 4 sts, O, T, K2.
Row 5   K1, T, * O, K5, P1, K3, O, T, K1, T. Rep from * to last 3 sts, O, T, K1.
Row 6   T, * O, K1, T, (O) twice, (T) twice, (O) twice, T, K2, O, T3. Rep from * to last 2 sts, O, T.
Row 7   K2, * O, T, K2, P1, K3, P1, T, O, K3. Rep from * to last 4 sts, T, O, K2.
Row 8   K3, * O, (T) twice, (O) twice, T, K1, T, O, K5. Rep from * to last 5 sts, T, O, K3.
Row 9   K4, * O, T, K2, P1, T, O, K7. Rep from * to last 6 sts, T, O, K4.
Row 10 K5, * O, T, K1, T, O, K9. Rep from * to last 7 sts, T, O, K5.
Row 11 K6, * O, T3, O, K11. Rep from * to last 8 sts, T, O, K6.

PLAIN HEXAGON

End with row 11 of the instructions for the 4-hole diamond.

Rows 12 to 15   As row 1.
Row 16 As row 2.
Row 17 As row 3.
Row 18 K2, T, * O, K7, O, T, K3, T. Rep from * to last 4 sts, O, T, K2.
Row 19 K1, T, * O, K9, O, T, K1, T. Rep from * to last 3 sts, O, T, K1.
Row 20 T, * O, K11, O, T3. Rep from * to last 2 sts, O, T.

Work rows 1 to 20 for an 'allover' pattern.

WAVES

Multiple of 14 sts plus 1.

Row 1 K5, T, * O, K1, O, T, K9, T. Rep from * to last 7 sts, O, T, K5.
Row 2 K4, T, * O, K3, O, T, K7, T. Rep from * to last 6 sts, O, T, K4
Row 3 K3, T, * O, K5, O, T, K5, T. Rep from * to last 5 sts, O, T, K3.
Row 4 K2, T, * O, K7, O, T, K3, T. Rep from * to last 4 sts, O, T, K2.
Row 5 K1, T, * O, K9, O, T, K1, T. Rep from * to last 3 sts, O, T, K1.
Row 6 T, * O, K11, O, T3. Rep from * to last 2 sts, O, T.

Rep rows 1 to 6.

Spider's Web, Lace Holes and Spider

Multiple of 10 sts plus 6.

SPIDER'S WEB

Row 1   K.
Row 2   K3, * T, O, K1, O, T, K5. Rep from * to last 3 sts, K3.
Row 3   K2, * T, O, K3, O, T, K3. Rep from * to last 2 sts, K2.
Row 4   K1, * (T, O) twice, K1, (O, T) twice, K1. Rep from * to end.
Row 5   (T, O) twice, * K3, O, T, O, T3, O, T, O. Rep from * to last 7 sts, K3, (O, T) twice.
Row 6   As row 4.
Row 7   As row 3.
Row 8   As row 2.
Row 9   K4, * O, STP, O, K7. Rep from * to last 4 sts, K4.
Row 10 K3, * O, T, K1, T, O, K5. Rep from * to last 3 sts, K3.
Row 11 K2, * O, T, O, STP, O, T, O, K3. Rep from * to last 2 sts, K2.
Row 12 K1, * (O, T) twice, K1, (T, O) twice, K1. Rep from * to end.
Row 13 As row 11.
Row 14 As row 10.
Row 15 As row 9.

LACE HOLES

Row 16 K to centre st, T, K to end.
Row 17 K.
Row 18 T, * (O) twice, (T) twice. Rep from * to last 2 sts, (O) twice, T.
Row 19 K2, * P1, K3. Rep from· * to last 2 sts, P1, K1.
Row 20 K2, * T, (O) twice, T. Rep from * to last 2 sts, K2.
Row 21 K4, * P1, K3. Rep from * to end.
Row 22 As row 18.
Row 23 As row 19.
Row 24 K to centre st, K twice into next st, K to end.
Row 25 K.

SPIDER PATTERN

Row 26 As row 2.
Row 27 As row 3.
Row 28 K3, * O, T, O, T3, O, K5. Rep from * to last 3 sts, K3.
Row 29 K3, * O, T, K1, T, O, K5. Rep from * to last 3 sts, K3.
Row 30 K4, * O, STP, O, K7. Rep from * to last 4 sts, K4.
Row 31 K4, * O, T3, O, K7. Rep from * to last 4 sts, K4.
80 **Row 32** K.

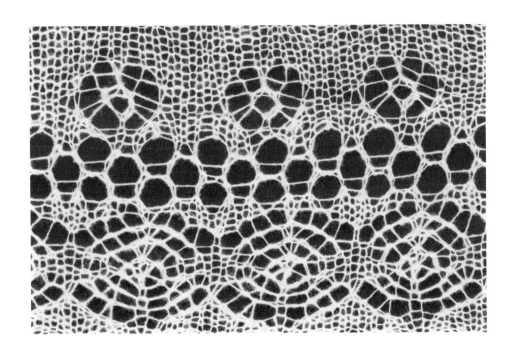

Cat's Paw

Multiple of 11 sts.

Row 1   K3, SKP, O, K1, O, T, K3
Rows 2, 4 and 6   P.
Row 3   K2, SKP, O, K3, O, T, K2.
Row 5   K4, O, T3, O, K4.
Row 7   K.
Row 8   P.

Rep rows 1 to 8.

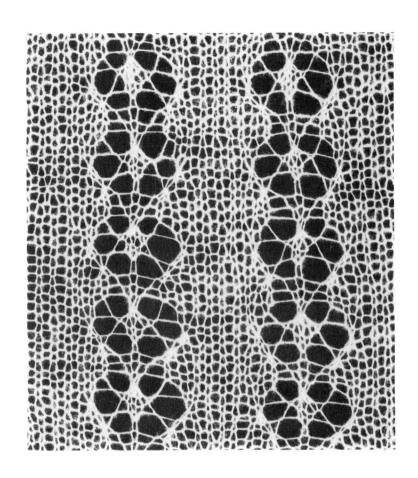

Arches and Columns

Multiple of 14 sts plus 1.

Rows 1 and 3 (wrong side)   P.
Row 2   T, O, * K3, O, K1, STP, K1, O, K3, O, STP, O. Rep from * to last 13 sts, K3, O, K1, STP, K1, O, K3, O, SKP.
Row 4   T, O, * K4, O, STP, O. Rep from * to last 6 sts, K4, O, SKP.

Rep rows 1 to 4.

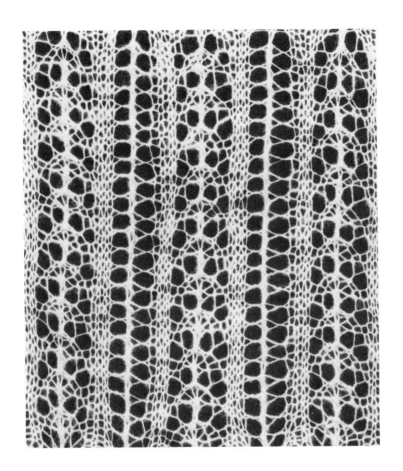

Peerie Flea

Multiple of 17 sts plus 6.
Work one row K.

Row 1   K3, * K7, O, STP, O, K7. Rep from * to last 3 sts, K3.
Row 2 and all foll alt rows   K.
Row 3   K3, * K5, T, O, K3, O, T, K5. Rep from * to last 3 sts, K3.
Row 5   K3, * K6, T, O, K1, O, T, K6. Rep from * to last 3 sts, K3.
Row 7   K3, * K3, O, STP, O, K5, O, STP, O, K3. Rep from * to last 3 sts, K3.
Row 9   K3, * K1, T, O, K3, O, T, K1, T, O, K3, O, T, K1. Rep from * to last 3 sts, K3.
Row 11   K3, * K2, T, O, K1, O, T, K3, T, O, K1, O, T, K2. Rep from * to last 3 sts, K3.
Row 13   K3, * K7, O, STP, O, K7. Rep from * to last 3 sts, K3.
Row 15   K3, * K5, T, O, K3, O, T, K5. Rep from * to last 3 sts, K3.
Row 17   K3, * K6, T, O, K1, O, T, K6. Rep from * to last 3 sts, K3.
Row 18 K.

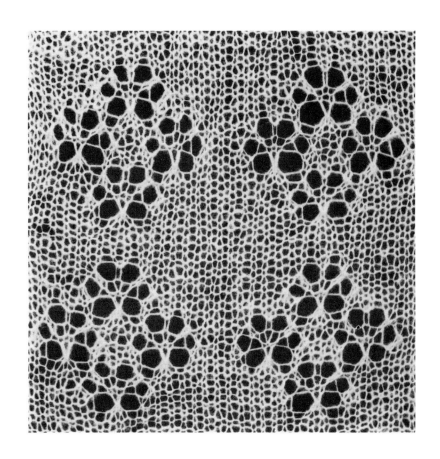

Diamond and Triangle

Cast on 50 sts.

Work across row 1 of left diamond panel, row 1 of centre panel and row 1 of right diamond panel and repeat this procedure for the following rows.

The number of rows over which one complete pattern is worked for the diamond and triangle patterns differs, therefore the instructions are given separately.

LEFT DIAMOND PANEL

Use 15 sts.
Row 1   K5, O, T, K5, O, T, K1.
Row 2 and all foll alt rows   P15.
Row 3   K3, T, O, K1, O, T, K3, T, O, K2.
Row 5   K2, T, O, K3, O, T, K3, O, T, K1.
Row 7   K1, T, O, K5, O, T, K1, T, O, K2.
Row 9   T, O, K7, O, T, K1, O, T, K1.
Row 11   K2, O, T, K3, T, O, K2, T, O, K2.
Row 13   K3, O, T, K1, T, O, K4, O, T, K1.
Row 15   K4, O, STP, O, K4, T, O, K2.
Row 16   P15.

Rep rows 1 to 16.

CENTRE PANEL

Use 20 sts.
Row 1   O, T, K16, T, O.
Row 2 and all foll alt rows   P20.
Row 3   K1, O, T, K14, T, O, K1.
Row 5   (O, T) twice, K12, (T, O) twice.
Row 7   K1, (O, T) twice, K10, (T, O) twice, K1.
Row 9   (O, T) three times, K8, (T, O) three times.
Row 11   K1, (O, T) three times, K6, (T, O) three times, K1.
Row 13   (O, T) four times, K4, (T, O) four times.
Row 15   K1, (O, T) four times, K2, (T, O) four times, K1.
Row 17   (O, T) five times, (T, O) five times.
Rows 19, 21 and 23   K20.
Row 24   P20.

Rep rows 1 to 24.

RIGHT DIAMOND PANEL

Use 15 sts.
Row 1   K1, T, O, K5, T, O, K5.
Row 2 and all foll alt rows   P15.
Row 3   K2, O, T, K3, T, O, K1, O, T, K3.
Row 5   K1, T, O, K3, T, O, K3, O, T, K2
Row 7   K2, O, T, K1, T, O, K5, O, T, K1.
Row 9   K1, T, O, K1, T, O, K7, O, T.
Row 11   K2, O, T, K2, O, T, K3, T, O, K2.
Row 13   K1, T, O, K4, O, T, K1, T, O, K3.
Row 15   K2, O, T, K4, O, STP, O, K4.
Row 16   P15.

Rep rows 1 to 16.

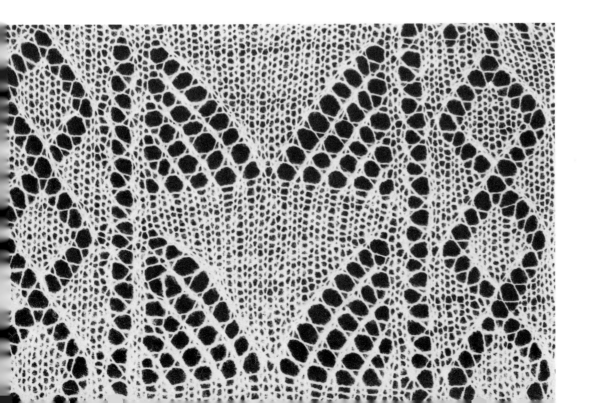

Rose Lace

Multiple of 20 sts plus 2.

Row 1   K1, * O, T3, O, K2, O, SKP, O, T3, O, K1, O, SKP, O, T3, O, K2, O, SKP. Rep from * to last st, K1.

Row 2 and all foll alt rows   P.

Row 3   K1, SKP, * O, K4, O, STP, O, K3, O, STP, O, K4, O, STP. Rep from * to last 6 sts, K6.

Row 5   K2, * (O, SKP) twice, K3, O, SKP, O, T3, O, K3, (T, O) twice, K1. Rep from * to end.

Row 7   * K3, (O, SKP) twice, K3, O, STP, O, K3, (T, O) twice. Rep from * to last 2 sts, K2.

Row 9   K4, * (O, SKP) twice, K7, (T, O) twice, K5. Rep from * to last 3 sts, K3.

Row 11   K5, * (O, SKP) twice, K5, (T, O) twice, K7. Rep from * to last 4 sts, K4.

Row 13   K6, * (O, SKP) twice, K3, (T, O) twice, K9. Rep from * to last 5 sts, K5.

Row 15   K2, * O, SKP, K3, (O, SKP) twice, K1, (T, O) twice, K3, T, O, K1. Rep from * to end.

Row 17   * (K3, O, SKP) twice, O, STP, O, T, O, K3, T, O. Rep from * to last 2 sts, K2.

Row 19   K1, * O, T3, O, K1, O, K3, T3, O, K1, O, STP, K3, O, K1, O, SKP. Rep from * to last st, K1.

Row 21   K1, SKP, * O, K3, O, K1, T3, O, K3, O, STP, K1, O, K3, O, STP. Rep from * to last 5 sts, K5.

Row 23   K2, * (O, SKP, O, T3, O, K2) twice, O, SKP, O, T3, O, K1. Rep from * to end.

Row 25   * K3, O, STP, (O, K4, O, STP) twice, O. Rep from * to last 2 sts, K2.

Row 27   K1, * O, T3, O, K3, (T, O) twice, K1, (O, SKP) twice, K3, O, SKP. Rep from * to last st, K1.

Row 29   K1, SKP, * O, K3, (T, O) twice, K3, (O, SKP) twice, K3, O, STP. Rep from * to last 5 sts, K5.

Row 31   K5, * (T, O) twice, K5, (O, SKP) twice, K7. Rep from * to last 4 sts, K4.

Row 33   K4, * (T, O) twice, K7, (O, SKP) twice, K5. Rep from * to last 3 sts, K3.

Row 35   * K3, (T, O) twice, K9, (O, SKP) twice. Rep from * to last 2 sts, K2.

Row 37   K2, * (T, O) twice, K3, T, O, K1, O, SKP, K3, (O, SKP) twice, K1. Rep from * to end.

Row 39   K1, T, * O, (T, O, K3) twice, O, SKP, K3, O, SKP, O, STP. Rep from * to last 2 sts, O, SKP.

Row 41   K2, * O, STP, K3, O, K1, O, SKP, O, T3, O, K1, O, K3, T3, O, K1. Rep from * to end.

Row 43   * K3, O, STP, K1, O, K3, O, STP, O, K3, O, K1, T3, O. Rep from * to last 2 sts, K2.

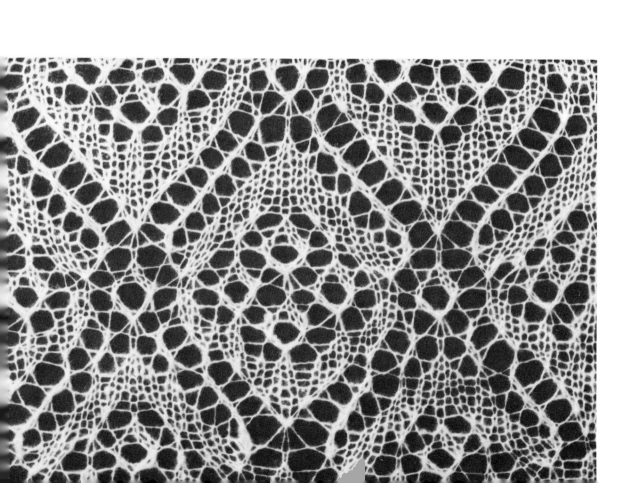

SHETLAND LACE GARMENTS

The patterns used in the following projects are my personal choice. Should you wish to substitute patterns given in the sample section, or indeed patterns used on other garments in this section, you should not find difficulty in doing so. With the aid of tension squares, samples of the patterns you choose, the diagrams given for the construction of shawls and stoles (pages 29 and 30) and details of the number of stitches over which the patterns repeat, you will be able to design garments which will be unique pieces of knitting.

To all dispersed sorts of arts and trades
I write the needles prayse (that never fades).
So long as children shall be got or borne,
So long as garments shall be made or worne,
So long as hemp or flax, or sheep shall bear
their linen woollen fleeces yeare by yeare,
So long as silk-wormes, with exhausted spoile,
of their own entrailes for man's gaine shall toyle,
Yea till the world be quite dissolv'd and past,
So long at least, the needles' use shall last.

The Prayse of the Needle.
John Taylor, the Water Poet, (1580–1653)

Baby's Shawl in Old Shale Pattern

MATERIALS

$6 \times \frac{1}{2}$ oz hanks of finest lace weight Shetland yarn.

NEEDLES

One pair 2-mm (no. 14) needles.

MEASUREMENTS

Approximately 107 cm (42 ins) square.

Cast on 13 sts and work one row in K.

LACE EDGING

** **Row 1**   K4, O, T, K1, O, (SKP, O) twice, K2.
Row 2   K2, (O, T) twice, O, K4, O, T, K2.
Row 3   K4, O, T, K3, O, (SKP, O) twice, K2.
Row 4   K2, (O, T) twice, O, K6, O, T, K2.
Row 5   K4, O, T, K5, O, (SKP, O) twice, K2.
Row 6   K2, (O, T) twice, O, K8, O, T, K2.
Row 7   K4, O, T, K7, O, (SKP, O) twice, K2.
Row 8   K2, (O, T) twice, O, K10, O, T, K2.
Row 9   K4, O, T, K9, O, (SKP, O) twice, K2.
Row 10 K1, (SKP, O) three times, T, K9, O, T, K2.
Row 11 K4, O, T, K6, SKP, (O, T) three times, K1.
Row 12 K1, (SKP, O) three times, T, K7, O, T, K2.
Row 13 K4, O, T, K4, SKP, (O, T) three times, K1.
Row 14 K1, (SKP, O) three times, T, K5, O, T, K2.
Row 15 K4, O, T, K2, SKP, (O, T) three times, K1.
Row 16 K1, (SKP, O) three times, T, K3, O, T, K2.
Row 17 K4, O, T, SKP, (O, T) three times, K1.
Row 18 K1, (SKP, O) three times, T, K1, O, T, K2.

Rep these 18 rows 14 times more. Cast off (15 scallops).

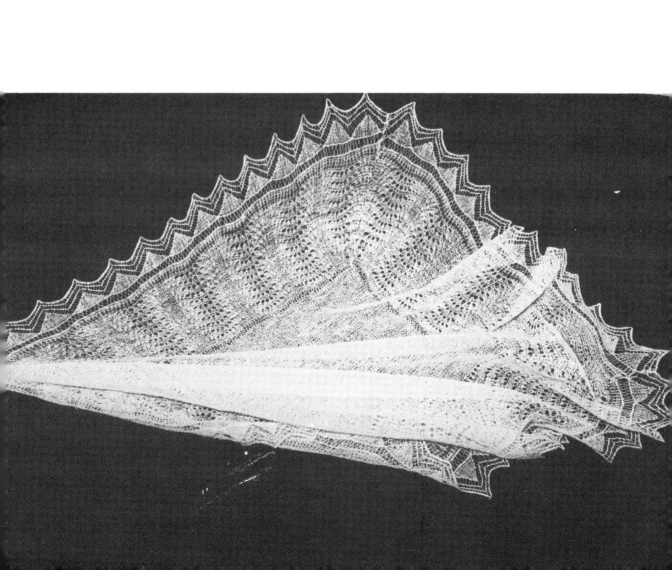

BORDER

Pick up and K 135 sts along straight side of lace edge, beginning at cast off edge, picking up 1 st for every other row of lace edge.

Rows 1, 2 and 3   K. ＊＊＊＊
Row 4   K1, ＊ K1, (T) three times, (O, K1) five times, O, (T) three times, K1. Rep from ＊ to last st, K1.
Rows 5 to 9   K.

Rep rows 4 to 9 inclusive five times more.

＊＊＊＊＊Now begin decreasing:

Row 1   (T) three times, T3, (O, K1) four times, O, (T) three times, K1, ＊ K1, (T) three times, (O, K1) five times, O, (T) three times, K1. Rep from ＊ four times more to last 20 sts, K1, (T) three times, (O, K1) four times, O, T3, (T) three times.

Rows 2 to 6   K.

Row 7   (T) twice, T3, (O, K1) three times, O, (T) three times, K1, ＊ K1, (T) three times, (O, K1) five times, O, (T) three times, K1. Rep from ＊ four times more to last 17 sts, K1, (T) three times, (O, K1) three times, O, T3, (T) twice.

Rows 8 to 12   K.

Row 13   T, T3, (O, K1) twice, O, (T) three times, K1, ＊ K1, (T) three times, (O, K1) five times, O, (T) three times, K1. Rep from ＊ four times more to last 14 sts, K1, (T) three times, (O, K1) twice, O, T3, T.

Rows 14 to 18   K.

Row 19   T3, O, K1, O, (T) three times, K1, ＊ K1, (T) three times, (O, K1) five times, O, (T) three times, K1. Rep from ＊ four times more to last 11 sts, K1, (T) three times, O, K1, O, T3.

Rows 20 to 24   K.

Row 25   T3, O, (T) twice, K1, ＊ K1, (T) three times, (O, K1) five times, O, (T) three times, K1. Rep from ＊ four times more to last 8 sts, K1, (T) twice, O, T3. (105 sts.)

Rows 26 to 32   K.

Row 33   K1, ＊ O, T. Rep from ＊ to end.

Row 34   K. ＊＊＊

CENTRE PIECE

Work in garter st (every row K) until centre is square. Leave sts on a spare needle.

Work three more borders from ** to *** and leave sts on spare needles. Graft sides of centre square (see pages 26 and 30).

Follow Dressing and Stretching instructions on page 18.

Hap Shawl in Old Shale Pattern

MATERIALS

4 oz lace weight Shetland yarn in white and 1 oz each of baby pink and baby blue.

NEEDLES

One pair 3.25-mm (no. 10) needles.

MEASUREMENTS

Approximately 127 cm (50 ins) square.

Follow the instructions for the Baby Shawl in Old Shale Pattern to ****, pages 94 to 97.
Work rows 4 to 9 as set using the following colours:
Rows 4 to 9   In pink.
Rows 4 to 9   In blue.
Rows 4 to 9 (twice)   In white.
Rows 4 to 9   In blue.
Rows 4 to 9   In pink.
Rows 4 to 9   In white.
Now follow instructions as set from *****.

Work centre in foll pattern.
Row 1   K1, * O, K2, STP, K2, O, K1. Rep from * to end.
Row 2 and all foll alt rows   K.
Row 3   K1, * K1, O, K1, STP, K1, O, K2. Rep from * to end.
Row 5   K1, * K2, O, STP, O, K3. Rep from * to end.
Row 7   T, * K2, O, K1, O, K2, STP. Rep from * to last 7 sts, K2, O, K1, O, K2, SKP.
Row 9   T, * K1, O, K3, O, K1, STP. Rep from * to last 7 sts, K1, O, K3, O, K1, SKP.
Row 11   T, * O, K5, O, STP. Rep from * to last 7 sts, O, K5, O, SKP.
Row 12   K.

Rep these 12 rows until centre piece is square (approximately 16 times) ending with rows 1 to 6.

Make three more borders following the instructions on page 98 and using the same colour sequence. Graft borders as shown on page 26 (diagram page 30). Follow Dressing and Stretching instructions on page 18.

This shawl is also lovely made in the natural colours of the Shetland sheep — in stripes of black, dark brown, beige and grey.

Baby's Shawl in Several Patterns

This pattern uses the tree, waves, strawberry and puzzle patterns.

MATERIALS

$9 \times \frac{1}{2}$ oz hanks finest lace weight Shetland yarn.

NEEDLES

One pair 1.5-mm (no. 16) needles. For a larger and looser shawl follow the pattern using larger needles. Needle sizes 1.75-mm, 2-mm or 2.25-mm (nos. 15, 14 or 13) may be used.

MEASUREMENTS

107 cm (42 ins) square.

LACE EDGING

** Cast on 14 sts and work one row in K.

Row 1   K3, O, T, K4, O, T, O, K3.
Row 2   O, T, K1, O, T, O, K4, T, O, K4.
Row 3   K2, T, O, K7, O, T, O, K3.
Row 4   O, T, K1, O, T, O, K1, O, T, K6, O, T, K1.
Row 5   K3, O, T, K3, T, O, K3, O, T, O, K3.
Row 6   O, T, K1, O, T, O, K5, O, T, K1, T, O, K4.
Row 7   K2, T, O, K5, O, T, K1, T, O, T, O, T, K2.
Row 8   O, (T) twice, O, T, O, T3, O, K7, O, T, K1.
Row 9   K3, O, T, K5, T, O, T, O, T, K2.
Row 10 O, (T) twice, O, T, O, T, K3, T, O, K4.
Row 11 K2, T, O, K4, T, O, T, O, T, K2.
Row 12 O, (T) twice, O, T, O, T, K4, O, T, K1.

Rep these 12 rows 40 times more (41 scallops). Cast off loosely.

BORDER

Pick up 246 sts along straight edge (6 sts to each scallop). Work three rows in K.

Tree

Row 4   K14, * O, T, K22. Rep from * to last 16 sts, O, T, K14.
Row 5   K to end.
Row 6   As row 4.
Row 7   K to end.
Row 8   As row 4.
Row 9   K to end.
Row 10 K10, * T, O, K2, O, T, K1, O, T, K15. Rep from * to last 11 sts, K11.
Row 11 K to end.
Row 12 K9, * T, O, K3, O, T, K2, O, T, K13. Rep from * to last 10 sts, K10.
Row 13 K to end.
Row 14 K8, * T, O, K4, O, T, K3, O, T, K11. Rep from * to last 9 sts, K9.
Row 15 K to end.
Row 16 K7, * T, O, K5, O, T, K4, O, T, K9. Rep from * to last 8 sts, K8.
Row 17 K7, * T, O, K13, O, T, K7. Rep from * to last 6 sts, K6.
Row 18 K5, * T, O, K3, T, O, K2, O, T, K1, O, T, K3, O, T, K5. Rep from * to last 6 sts, K6.
Row 19 K5, *T, O, K17, O, T, K3. Rep from * to last 4 sts, K2, T.
Row 20 K8, * T, O, K3, O, T, K2, O, T, K13. Rep from * to last 10 sts, K8, T.
Row 21 K to last 2 sts, T.
Row 22 K6, * T, O, K4, O, T, K3, O, T, K11. Rep from * to last 10 sts, K6, (T)2.
Row 23 K to last 2 sts, T.
Row 24 K4, * T, O, K5, O, T, K4, O, T, K9. Rep from * to last 6 sts, K4, T.
Row 25 K4, * T, O, K13, O, T, K7. Rep from * to last 3 sts, K1, T.
Row 26 K1, * T, O, K3, T, O, K2, O, T, K1, O, T, K3, O, T, K5. Rep from * to last 3 sts, K1, T.
Row 27 K to last 2 sts, T.
Row 28 K4, * T, O, K3, O, T, K2, O, T, K13. Rep from * to last 6 sts, K4, T.
Row 29 K to last 2 sts, T.
Row 30 K2, * T, O, K4, O, T, K3, O, T, K11. Rep from * to last 4 sts, K2, T.
Row 31 K2, * T, O, K11, O, T, K9. Rep from * to last 3 sts, STP.
Row 32 K7, O, T, * K5, O, T, K7, T, O, K6, O, T. Rep from * to last 8 sts, K5, O, STP.
Row 33 K to end.
Row 34 K3, * T, O, K2, O, T, K1, O, T, K15. Rep from * to last 4 sts, K2, T.
Row 35 K to last 2 sts, T.
Row 36 K1, * T, O, K3, O, T, K2, O, T, K13. Rep from * to last 4 sts, (T) twice.
Row 37 K to last 2 sts, T.
Row 38 K5, * O, T, K3, O, T, K11, T, O, K4. Rep from * to last 7 sts, O, T, K3, T.
Row 39 K11, * O, T, K9, T, O, K11. Rep from * to last 11 sts, K9, T.

Row 40 K4, * O, T, K5, O, T, K7, T, O, K6. Rep from * to last 6 sts, O, T, K2, T.

Row 41 K to last 2 sts, T.

Row 42 K1, * T, O, K1, O, T, K19. Rep from * to last 7 sts, T, O, K1, O, (T) twice.

Row 43 * T, O, K3, O, T, K17. Rep from * to last 7 sts, T, O, K3, O, T.

Row 44 K to last 2 sts, T.

Row 45 K3, T, O, K19, * O, T, O, STP, O, K19. Rep from * to last 6 sts,
O, T, O, STP, K1.

Row 46 K3, T, O, * K19, O, T, K1, T, O. Rep from * to last 5 sts, O, T, K1, T.

Row 47 K1, T, O, K21, * O, STP, O, K21. Rep from * to last 4 sts, O, STP, K1.

Waves

Rows 48 and 49 K to last 2 sts, T.

Row 50 K to end (217 sts).

Row 51 K11, * O, STP, O, K21. Rep from * to last 11 sts, K9, T.

Row 52 K8, * T, O, K3, O, T, K17. Rep from * to last 11 sts, O, T, K7, T.

Row 53 K7, * T, O, K5, O, T, K15. Rep from * to last 7 sts, K5, T.

Row 54 K5, * T, O, K7, O, T, K13. Rep from * to last 6 sts, K4, T.

Row 55 K4, * T, O, K9, O, T, K11. Rep from * to last 4 sts, K2, T.

Row 56 K2, * T, O, K3, T, (O) twice, T, K4, O, T, K9. Rep from * to
last 3 sts, K1, T.

Row 57 K1, * T, O, K7, P1, K5, O, T, K7. Rep from * to last 3 sts, O, STP.

Row 58 K4, * T, (O) twice, (T) twice, (O) twice, T, K4, O, T, K5, T, O, K3. Rep from
* to last 2 sts, T.

Row 59 * K7, P1, K3, P1, K5, O, T, K3, T, O. Rep from * to last 5 sts, K3, T.

Row 60 K1, * T, (O) twice, T, K4, T, (O) twice, T, K4, O, T, K1, T, O, K3. Rep from
* to last 3 sts, K1, T.

Row 61 K3, * K1, P1, K7, P1, K5, O, STP, O, K6. Rep from * to last 2 sts, T.

Row 62 K10, * T, (O) twice, T, K8, T, (O) twice, T, K8. Rep from * to
last 4 sts, K2, T.

Row 63 K6, * O, STP, O, K4, P1, K11, P1, K4. Rep from * to last 4 sts, K2, T.

Row 64 K1, T, * O, K3, O, T, K3, T, (O) twice, T, K4, T, (O) twice, T, K2, T. Rep
from * to last 4 sts, K2, T.

Row 65 K2, T, * O, K5, O, T, K3, P1, K7, P1, K3, T. Rep from * to last 2 sts, T.

Row 66 K7, O, T, * K3, T, (O) twice, (T) twice, (O) twice, T, K2, T, O, K7, O, T.
Rep from * to last 3 sts, STP.

Row 67 K10, O, T, * K3, P1, K3, P1, K3, T, O, K9, O, T. Rep from * to
last 8 sts, K6, T.

Row 68 K8, * O, T, K3, T, (O) twice, T, K2, T, O, K11. Rep from * to
last 11 sts, K9, T.

Row 69 K11, * O, T, K3, P1, K3, T, O, K13. Rep from * to last 9 sts, K7, T.

Row 70 K9, * O, T, K5, T, O, K15. Rep from * to last 12 sts, K10, T.

Row 71 K12, * O, T, K3, T, O, K17. Rep from * to last 10 sts, K8, T.

Row 72 K10, * O, T, K1, T, O, K19. Rep from * to last 13 sts, K11, T.

Row 73 K13, * O, STP, O, K21. Rep from * to last 11 sts, K9, T.

Strawberry

Rows 74 and 75   K to last 2 sts, T.

Row 76   K to last 2 sts, T (191 sts).

Row 77   K24, * O, T, K22. Rep from * to last 21 sts, K19, T.

Row 78   K to last 2 sts, T.

Row 79   K21, * T, O, K1, O, T, K19. Rep from * to last 19 sts, K17, T.

Row 80   K to last 2 sts, T.

Row 81   K19, * T, O, K3, O, T, K17. Rep from * to last 17 sts, K15, T.

Row 82   K to last 2 sts, T.

Row 83   K20, * O, STP, O, K21. Rep from * to last 18 sts, K16, T.

Row 84   K to last 2 sts, T.

Row 85   * K17, O, T, K3, T, O. Rep from * to last 15 sts, K13, T.

Row 86   K to last 2 sts, T.

Row 87   K14, * T, O, K1, O, T, K1, T, O, K1, O, T, K13. Rep from * to last 12 sts, K10, T.

Row 88   K to last 2 sts, T.

Row 89   K12, * T, O, K3, O, STP, O, K3, O, T, K11. Rep from * to last 10 sts, K8, T.

Row 90   K to last 2 sts, T.

Row 91   K13, * O, STP, O, K3, O, STP, O, K15. Rep from * to last 11 sts, K9, T.

Row 92   K to last 2 sts, T.

Row 93   K16, * O, T, K10. Rep from * to last 13 sts, K11, T.

Row 94   K to last 2 sts, T.

Row 95   K13, * T, O, K1, O, T, K7. Rep from * to last 11 sts, K9, T.

Row 96   K to last 2 sts, T.

Row 97   K11, * T, O, K3, O, T, K5. Rep from * to last 9 sts, K7, T.

Row 98   K to last 2 sts, T.

Row 99   K12, * O, STP, O, K9. Rep from * to last 10 sts, K8, T.

Row 100   K to last 2 sts, T.

Row 101   K9, * O, T, K3, T, O, K5. Rep from * to last 2 sts, T.

Row 102   * K7, O, T, K1, T, O. Rep from * to last 10 sts, K8, T.

Row 103   K to last 2 sts, T.

Row 104   K7, * O, STP, O, K9. Rep from * to last 10 sts, K8, T.

Rows 105 to 107   K to last 2 sts, T.

Row 108   K2, * O, T. Rep from * to end.

Row 109   K to last 2 sts, T.

Rows 110 and 111   K to end (159 sts).***

CENTRE

Rows 109 to 111 of the border form the first three rows of the centre.

Row 4   K7, * O, T, K6. Rep from * to end.
Row 5   K to end.
Row 6   K6, * O, STP, O, K5. Rep from * to last st, K1.
Row 7   K to end.
Row 8   K5, * O, T, K1, T, O, K3. Rep from * to last 2 sts, K2.
Row 9   K6, * O, STP, O, K5. Rep from * to last st, K1.
Row 10 K to end.
Row 11 K4, * O, T, K3, T, O, K1. Rep from * to last 3 sts, K3.
Row 12 K5, * O, T, K1, T, O, K3. Rep from * to last 2 sts, K2.
Row 13 K6, * O, STP, O, K5. Rep from * to last st, K1.
Row 14 K to end.
Row 15 K4, * T, O, K3, O, T, K1. Rep from * to last 3 sts, K3.
Row 16 K2, T, O, * K5, O, STP, O. Rep from * to last 10 sts, K5, O, T, K3.

Rep rows 4 to 16 inclusive until centre is square, ending with a row 10. Work one row in K. Leave sts in a spare needle.

Work three more borders from ** to *** leaving sts on spare needles.

Graft borders together (see page 26).

Follow Dressing and Stretching instructions on page 18.

Semicircular Scarf in Spider Pattern

MATERIALS

$3 \times \frac{1}{2}$ oz hanks of finest lace weight Shetland yarn.

NEEDLES

One pair 2-mm (no. 14) needles.

MEASUREMENTS

Depth approximately 38 cm (15 ins), length of long side 76 cm (30 ins).

LACE   EDGING

Cast on 12 sts.

Row 1	K3, O, T, K1, (T, O) twice, K2.
Row 2	K2, O, T, O, K5, O, T, K1.
Row 3	K3, O, T, K4, O, T, O, K2.
Row 4	K2, O, T, O, K7, O, T, K1.
Row 5	K3, O, (T) twice, (O) twice, T, U, T, O, T, O, K2.
Row 6	K2, O, T, O, K5, P1, K3, O, T, K1.
Row 7	K3, O, T, K2, T, (O) twice, T, (T, O) twice, K2.
Row 8	K1, (T, O) twice, T, K1, P1, K5, O, T, K1.
Row 9	K3, O, (T) twice, (O) twice, T, (T, O) twice, T, K1.
Row 10	K1, (T, O) twice, T, K1, P1, K3, O, T, K1.
Row 11	K3, O, T, K2, (T, O) twice, T, K1.
Row 12	K1, (T, O) twice, T, K3, O, T, K1.

Work these 12 rows 37 times.

Cast off very loosely.

MAIN   PART

Note: Take extra care to work the edge stitches more loosely than usual to enable these edges to have enough elasticity to overcome the pulling effect of the decreases.

Cast on 263 sts loosely and work one row in K.

Row 1	K2, T, O, K3, O, * STP, O, K3, O. Rep from * to last 4 sts, T, K2.
Row 2	K2, * K1, O, T, K1, T, O. Rep from * to last 3 sts, K3.
Row 3	K3, * O, STP, O, T, O, K1. Rep from * to last 2 sts, K2.
Row 4	K2, * K1, O, T, K1, T, O. Rep from * to last 3 sts, K3.
Row 5	K4, * O, STP, O, K3. Rep from * to last st, K1.

Row 6   K2, * K1, T, O, K1, O, T. Rep from * to last 3 sts, K3.

Row 7   K3, * T, O, K1, O, STP, O. Rep from * to last 2 sts, K2.

Row 8   K2, * K1, T, O, K1, O, T. Rep from * to last 3 sts, K3.
             Rep these last 8 rows twice more.

Row 25   K2, (STP) twice, T, O, K3, O, * STP, O, K3, O. Rep from * to last 10 sts, O, STP, T, STP, K2.

Row 26   K2, STP, O, T, K1, T, O, * K1, O, T, K1, T, O. Rep from * to last 5 sts, STP, K2.

Rows 27 to 32   Work as rows 3 to 8.

Rows 33 to 40 Work as rows 1 to 8.

Rep rows 25 to 40 three times more (215 sts).

Now work rows 25 to 32 only, until there are 71 sts.

Work rows 1 to 8 *but* cast off 6 sts at the beginning of each row until there are 23 sts.

Next row   K2, STP, K to last 5 sts, STP, K2.

Work this row twice more.

Cast off extremely loosely.

Graft straight edge of lace edge to curved edge of the main part (see page 26).

Follow Dressing and Stretching instructions on page 18.

This is a copy of a scarf found in an old box of knitting discovered recently at Uyeasound, Unst. As the original scarf was black, you may like to dye it with a cold water dye suitable for woollen fabrics.

Scarf in Cockleshell Pattern

MATERIALS

2 oz of lace weight Shetland wool in main colour and $\frac{1}{2}$ oz hanks in each of two contrasting colours.

NEEDLES

One pair 3.25-mm (no. 10) needles.

MEASUREMENTS

Approximately 107 cm (42 ins) long.

Using main colour cast on 71 sts loosely and work one row in K.

Row 1   K2, T, O, P3, * (O) twice, PT, K13, PT, (O) twice, P3. Rep from * to last 4 sts, O, T, K2.

Row 2   K2, T, O, * K4, P1, K16, P1. Rep from * to last 7 sts, K3, O, T, K2.

Row 3   K2, T, O, * P3, K19. Rep from * to last 7 sts, P3, O, T, K2.

Row 4   K2, T, O, * K to last 4 sts, O, T, K2.

Row 5   K2, T, O, P3, * ([O] twice, PT) twice, K11, (PT, [O] twice) twice, P3. Rep from * to last 4 sts, O, T, K2.

Row 6   K2, T, O, * K4, P1, K2, P1, K14, P1, K2, P1. Rep from * to last 7 sts, K3, O, T, K2.

Row 7   K2, T, O, * P3, K23. Rep from * to last 7 sts, P3, O, T, K2.

Change to first contrast colour.

Row 8   K2, T, O, K7, * ([O] twice, K1) 14 times, K12. Rep from * to last 11 sts, K7, O, T, K2.

Row 9   K2, T, O, P3, * ([O] twice, PT) twice, (O) twice, drop 14 loops between the next 15 sts and P these 15 sts tog (making one single st), ([O] twice, PT) twice, (O) twice, P3. Rep from * to last 4 sts, O, T, K2.

Change to main colour.

Row 10 K2, T, O, * K4, (P1, K2) five times, P1. Rep from * to last 7 sts, K3, O, T, K2.

Row 11 K2, T, O, * P3, K17. Rep from * to last 7 sts, P3, O, T, K2.

Row 12 K2, T, O, * K to last 4 sts, O, T, K2.

These 12 rows form the pattern. Work rows 8 and 9 in the contrasting colours. alternately. Repeat these 12 rows 12 times.

Leave sts in a spare needle and work a second piece, repeating the instructions from the beginning of the pattern. Graft the two pieces together (see page 26).

Follow Dressing and Stretching instructions on page 18.

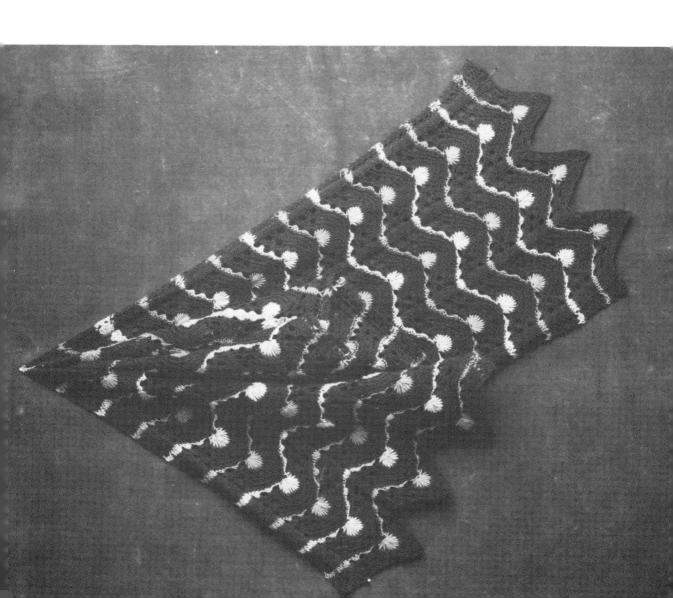

Hap Scarf in New Shale Pattern

MATERIALS

2 oz of lace weight Shetland yarn in beige (202) and $\frac{1}{4}$ oz oddments of each of the following colours:

pale green (26)   dark blue (48)
dark green (25)   pale orange (90)
pale blue (75)   pink (95)

MEASUREMENTS

Approximately 117 cm (46 ins) long.

NEEDLES

One pair 4-mm (no. 8) needles.

Using beige yarn cast on 65 sts.
The following two rows form pattern:

Row 1   K2, T, * K3, O, K1, O, K3, T3. Rep from * to last 11 sts, K3, O, K1, O, K3, T, K2.
Row 2   K.

Rep these two rows in the following colour order:
36 rows beige
6 rows dark green
8 rows beige
2 rows pale blue
2 rows pale orange
2 rows pale blue
8 rows beige
6 rows dark green
12 rows beige
2 rows dark blue
12 rows beige
2 rows pale green
2 rows pink
2 rows pale green
12 rows beige
2 rows dark blue
12 rows beige
6 rows dark green

* 8 rows beige
2 rows pale blue
2 rows pale orange
2 rows pale blue

Rep from and include * 8 rows beige and work colours in reverse order ending with 26 rows beige.
Cast off loosely.

Follow Dressing and Stretching instructions on page 18.

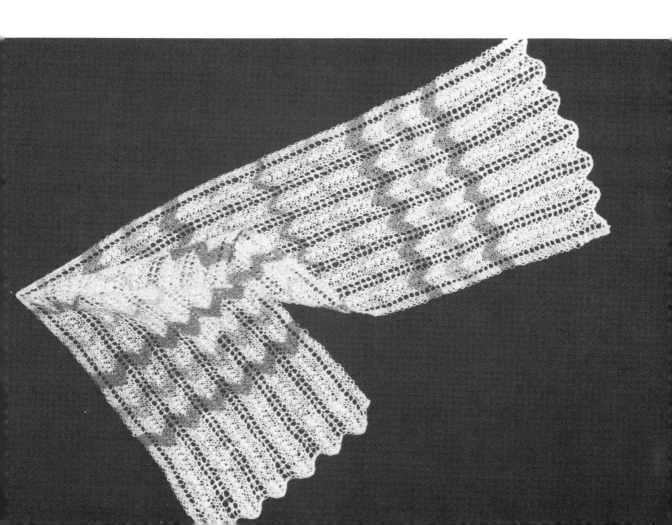

Baby's Christening Dress

MATERIALS

$4 \times \frac{1}{2}$ oz hanks finest lace weight Shetland yarn.

NEEDLES

3×2-mm (no. 14) needles.

MEASUREMENTS

To fit up to a 56 cm (22 in) chest.

TENSION

Eight stitches to 2.5 cm (1 in) over garter stitch when washed and stretched (your tension square should be at least 13 cm square). Because this is a fitted garment, it is important that you knit a tension square.

Note: A scalloped pattern such as old shale could be easily substituted here in place of the pattern used.

FIRST SKIRT

Bead Stitch and Lace Hole Edging

∗ Cast on 18 sts and work one row in K.

Row 1   K3, O, T, O, K1, T, (O) twice, (T) twice, O, K1, T, O, T, K1.
Row 2   K2, O, K1, T, O, K4, P1, T, O, K3, O, T, K1.
Row 3   K3, O, T, K2, O, (T) twice, (O) twice, T, K1, O, T, K1, O, K2.
Row 4   K2, O, K1, T, O, K4, P1, T, O, K1, T, K2, O, T, K1.
Row 5   K3, O, T, K3, O, (T) twice, (O) twice, T, K1, O, T, K1, O, K2.
Row 6   K2, O, K1, T, O, K4, P1, T, O, K1, O, T, K3, O, T, K1.
Row 7   K3, O, (T) twice, O, K3, O, (T) twice, (O) twice, T, K1, O, T, K1, O, K2.
Row 8   K2, O, K1, T, O, K4, P1, T, O, K5, (O, T, K1) twice.
Row 9   K3, O, T, K1, O, T, K1, T, O, K1, O, (T) twice, (O) twice, T, K1,
            O, T, K1, O, K2.
Row 10   K2, O, K1, T, O, K4, P1, T, O, K3, O, STP, O, K4, O, T, K1.
Row 11   K3, O, T, K2, T, O, K5, O, (T) twice, (O) twice, T, K1, O, T, K1, O, K2.
Row 12   K1, T, O, T, K1, O, T, K1, P1, K3, O, T, K1, T, O, K1, O, T, K3, O, T, K1.
Row 13   K3, O, (T) twice, O, K3, O, STP, O, K1, T, (O) twice, (T) twice, O, K1,
            T, O, T, K1.

Row 14 K1, T, O, T, K1, O, T, K1, P1, K3, O, T, K4, (O, T, K1) twice.

Row 15 K3, O, T, K1, O, T, K1, T, O, K1, T, (O) twice, (T) twice, O, K1, T, O, T, K1.

Row 16 K1, T, O, T, K1, O, T, K1, P1, K3, O, STP, O, K4, O, T, K1.

Row 17 K3, O, T, K2, T, O, K1, T, (O) twice, (T) twice, O, K1, T, O, T, K1.

Row 18 K1, T, O, T, K1, O, T, K1, P1, K3, O, T, K3, O, T, K1.

Row 19 K3, O, (T) twice, O, K1, T, (O) twice, (T) twice, O, K1, T, O, T, K1.

Row 20 K1, T, O, T, K1, O, T, K1, P1, K3, (O, T, K1) twice.

Rep rows 1 to 20 until there are 20 scallops. Cast off loosely.

Pick up and K 204 sts evenly along straight edge of lace edge (1 st from every other row of lace edge plus 2 extra sts at each end). **

Lace Holes

Rows 1 and 2 K.

Row 3 K1, * T, O. Rep from * to last st, K1.

Row 4 K.

Row 5 As row 3.

Rows 6 and 7 K.

Half Madeiras

Row 8 K2, * T, O, K5. Rep from * to last 6 sts, T, O, K4.

Row 9 * K3, (O, T) twice. Rep from * to last st, K1.

Row 10 K2, * (T, O) twice, K3. Rep from * to last 6 sts, (T, O) twice, K2.

Row 11 * K1, (O, T) three times. Rep from * to last st, K1.

Row 12 K2, * (T, O) three times, K1. Rep from * to last 6 sts, (T, O) twice, K2.

Row 13 * K1, (O, T) three times. Rep from * to last st, K1.

Row 14 K2, * (T, O) twice, K3. Rep from * to last 6 sts, (T, O) twice, K2.

Row 15 * K3, (O, T) twice. Rep from * to last st, K1.

Row 16 K2, * T, O, K5. Rep from * to last 6 sts, T, O, K4.

Row 17 * K5, O, T. Rep from * to last st, K1.

Rows 18 and 19 K.

Lace Holes

Row 20 As row 3.

Rows 21 and 22 K.

Zigzag of Madeiras

Row 23 K2, * K1, O, STP, O, K24. Rep from * to last 5 sts, O, STP, O, K2.

114 **Row 24** K1, * O, T, K1, T, O, K23. Rep from * to last 7 sts, O, T, K1, T, O, K2.

Row 25 K1, * O, T, O, STP, O, T, O, K21. Rep from * to last 7 sts, O, T, O, STP, O, K2.

Row 26 K1, * O, T, K1, (T, O) twice, K1, T, O, K12, T, O, K2, O, T. Rep from * to last 7 sts, O, T, K1, T, O, K2.

Row 27 K1, * O, T, O, STP, O, T, O, K2, O, STP, O, K11, O, STP, O, K2. Rep from * to last 7 sts, O, T, O, STP, O, K2.

Row 28 * K1, O, T, K1, T, O, K2, O, T, K1, T, O, K9, O, T, K1, T, O, K1. Rep from * to last 8 sts, K1, O, T, K1, T, O, K2.

Row 29 K1, * K2, O, STP, O, K2, O, T, O, STP, O, T, O, K7, O, T, O, STP, O, T, O. Rep from * to last 7 sts, K2, O, STP, O, K2.

Row 30 K6, * (O, T) twice, K1, (T, O) twice, K5. Rep from * to last 2 sts, K2.

Row 31 K2, * K6, O, T, O, STP, O, T, O, K3, O, T, K2, O, T, O, STP, O, T, O, K1. Rep from * to last 6 sts, K6.

Row 32 K6, * K2, O, T, K1, T, O, K3, O, STP, O, K3, O, T, K1, T, O, K7. Rep from * to last 2 sts, K2.

Row 33 K2, * K8, O, STP, O, K3, O, T, K1, T, O, K3, O, STP, O, K3. Rep from * to last 6 sts, K6.

Row 34 K6, * K8, O, T, O, STP, O, T, O, K13. Rep from * to last 2 sts, K2.

Row 35 K2, * K12, (O, T) twice, K1, (T, O) twice, K7. Rep from * to last 6 sts, K6.

Row 36 K6, * K8, O, T, O, STP, O, T, O, K13. Rep from * to last 2 sts, K2.

Row 37 K2, * K14, O, T, K1, T, O, K9. Rep from * to last 6 sts, K6.

Row 38 K2, * K14, O, STP, O, K11. Rep from * to last 6 sts, K6.

Row 39 K.

Waves

Row 40 K2, * K13, T, O, K1, O, T, K10. Rep from * to last 6 sts, K6.

Row 41 K2, * K13, T, O, K3, O, T, K8. Rep from * to last 6 sts, K6.

Row 42 K2, * K11, T, O, K5, O, T, K8. Rep from * to last 6 sts, K6.

Row 43 K2, * K11, T, O, K7, O, T, K6. Rep from * to last 6 sts, K6.

Row 44 K2, * K9, T, O, K9, O, T, K6. Rep from * to last 6 sts, K6.

Row 45 K2, * K9, T, O, K11, O, T, K4. Rep from * to last 6 sts, K6.

Row 46 K2, * K7, T, O, K13, O, T, K4. Rep from * to last 6 sts, K6.

Row 47 K2, * K7, T, O, K15, O, T, K2. Rep from * to last 6 sts, K6.

Row 48 K2, * K5, T, O, K17, O, T, K2. Rep from * to last 6 sts, K6.

Row 49 K2, * K5, T, O, K19, O, T. Rep from * to last 6 sts, K6.

Row 50 K5, * T, O, K21, O, T, K3. Rep from * to last 3 sts, K3.

Row 51 K5, * T, O, K23, O, T, K1. Rep from * to last 3 sts, K3.

Row 52 K3, T, O, * K25, O, STP, O. Rep from * to last 31 sts, K25, O, T, K4. ***

Work 136 rows in K and leave sts on a spare needle.

SECOND SKIRT

Work lace edging as for first skirt from * but work until there are 23 scallops. Pick up and K 232 sts along straight edge of lace edge (1 st from every other row of lace edge plus 1 extra st at each end). Work as for first skirt from ** to ***. Now work 44 rows in K.

Both skirts are dressed at this stage.

Remove sts of first skirt from needle and thread a strong white yarn through sts leaving long ends. Rep for second skirt. Follow Dressing and Stretching instructions on page 18. When dry replace sts from first skirt on to needle. Rep for second skirt and second needle.

FIRST SKIRT

Rejoin yarn to appropriate edge of work.
Next row   K3, * T, K1. Rep from * to last 3 sts, K3. (138 sts.)
Work 3 rows in K. Break off yarn.

SECOND SKIRT

Rejoin yarn to appropriate edge of work.

Next row   K7, * T, K1, (T) twice. Rep from * to last 8 sts, T, K6. (138 sts.)

Place first skirt behind second skirt with right sides of work facing you. Hold both sets of sts on both needles together in your left hand. With a third needle and yarn, knit together the first st from each needle and slip it on to the right-hand needle. Rep this procedure for the rest of the sts, thus knitting the two skirts together in a single row of sts on to the right-hand needle. Continue on these 138 sts for the yoke.

YOKE

Lace Holes

Row 1   K1, * T, O. Rep from * to last 2 sts, K2.
Rows 2 and 4   K.
Row 3   As row 1.

Divide for Front and Back Yoke

Next row   K30, cast off next 9 sts loosely, K60, cast off next 9 sts loosely, K30.
   Continue on the last 30 sts knitted for back yoke.

FIRST BACK YOKE

**** Continue in K and decrease 1 st at armhole edge only on the second and every foll alt row until there are 27 sts. Work in K for a further 36 rows.

Next row Cast off 6 sts (neck edge), work to end.

Decrease 1 st at neck edge only on the second and foll alt rows until there are 18 sts. Work a further 4 rows. Leave sts on a holder.

SECOND BACK YOKE

Rejoin yarn to armhole edge of the 30 sts for the second back yoke. Work as for the first yoke from ****. Leave sts on a holder.

FRONT YOKE

Rejoin yarn to remaining 60 sts and work 1 row in K. Continue in K and decrease 1 st at each end of next and every foll alt row until there are 54 sts. Work a further 28 rows.

Begin neck shaping

Next row K22, cast off next 10 sts loosely, K22. *****
   Continue on the last 22 sts knitted for the first shoulder. Decrease 1 st at neck edge only on next and every foll third row until there are 18 sts. Work until front yoke matches back yoke in length and leave sts on a holder.
   Rejoin yarn to neck edge of remaining 22 sts and work as for first shoulder from *****. Leave sts on a holder.
   Place sts from shoulders on to strong yarn. Dampen front and back yokes only and stretch and dry as shown on page 26. This must be done extremely carefully, keeping the skirts away from the pins. When dry graft shoulders as shown on page 26.

SLEEVES

Follow instructions for bead stitch and lace hole edging from * and work until there are 5 scallops. Cast off loosely. Follow Dressing and Stretching instructions page 18.

Graft the straight edge of the lace edge to the armhole (see page 26). Now graft half the cast on and cast off ends of the sleeve to the base of the armhole (the cast off sts of the yoke above the rows of lace holes). Graft the remaining ends of the sleeve together.

Graft the back seam of the first skirt only (see page 26) to 10 cm (4 in) below the lace holes at the yoke. Make button loops and sew on buttons.

Make sure all ends are secure and weave into back of work.